Praise for Raised Right

W9-BWX-707

"Journalist [Alisa] Harris gives a face and a voice to America's younger generation, offering herself up as a case study of Christian youth caught in a partisan nation.… Young Americans will identify with her coming-of-age struggles and passion for weeding out injustice. Right-wing politicians and older generations of Christians should pay close attention in order to understand, and perhaps empathize with, her demographic."

—*Publishers Weekly*

"A wonderful story for political misfits of all shapes and colors. Harris invites you to hop off the political bandwagon and to walk with her down the narrow way that leads to life. And she reminds you not to veer too far off the path to the left or to the right, lest you get confused and can't find the way home again."

> —SHANE CLAIBORNE, author, activist, and recovering sinner, www.thesimpleway.org

"*Raised Right* demonstrates that the evangelical stampede to the far right in the 1980s has produced a generational backlash, as young evangelicals like Alisa Harris encounter the Hebrew prophets and the words of Jesus. This is the most encouraging book about evangelicals and politics I have read in a very long time."

> —RANDALL BALMER, Columbia University, author of *Thy Kingdom Come: How the Religious Right Distorts the Faith and Threatens America*

"*Raised Right* is funny, insightful, and packed with truth. Harris speaks on behalf of a generation of culture warriors longing for a more peaceful way forward. Those who grew up in the trenches will relate to every page."

> —RACHEL HELD EVANS, author of *Evolving in Monkey Town*

Valparaiso Public Library
103 Jefferson Street
Valparaiso, IN 46383

"In *Raised Right*, Alisa Harris paints a fascinating picture of how the same religious devotion can send succeeding generations to opposite sides of the political battlefield. And while her story may be more common than ever, it's uncommonly told. Alisa's voice is fresh, honest, gracious, and provocative in all the right places. An enthralling and illuminating read."

—JASON BOYETT, author of *O Me of Little Faith: True Confessions of a Spiritual Weakling*

"Alisa Harris is a smart, fearless, gracious writer who, in her memoir *Raised Right*, showcases a deft mature-beyond-her-years honesty and kindness when sharing her affecting story of growing up in a politics-and-faith-charged environment. But the brilliance of *Raised Right* shines brightest when Harris begins confessing—often with a self-deprecating spin—the personal and spiritual unraveling that happens when she begins to unmarry her faith from her politics. Ultimately, hope wins throughout as Harris discovers small bits of humble truth along the journey. And because narrative in *Raised Right* is rich yet familiar, readers will discover small bits of their own."

—MATTHEW PAUL TURNER, author of *Churched* and *Hear No Evil*

"*Raised Right* chronicles Alisa Harris's journey from an evangelical childhood community steeped in the politics of James Dobson to an evangelical young adulthood where the politics of Barack Obama are preferred. It is engaging and well written, and it will be very illuminating to anyone who wants to understand the changes afoot among youth raised evangelical and what those changes will mean for American politics."

—JONATHAN DUDLEY, author of *Broken Words: The Abuse of Science and Faith in American Politics*

RAISED RIGHT

RAISED RIGHT

How I Untangled
My Faith
from
Politics

PORTER COUNTY PUBLIC LIBRARY

Valparaiso Public Library
103 Jefferson Street
Valparaiso, IN 46383

ALISA HARRIS

WATERBROOK
PRESS

NF   277.3083 HAR   VAL
Harris, Alisa.
Raised right : how I untangled
33410011299627   OCT   8 2011

RAISED RIGHT
PUBLISHED BY WATERBROOK PRESS
12265 Oracle Boulevard, Suite 200
Colorado Springs, Colorado 80921

All Scripture quotations, unless otherwise indicated, are taken from the New King James Version®. Copyright © 1982 by Thomas Nelson Inc. Used by permission. All rights reserved. Scripture quotations marked (KJV) are taken from the King James Version. Scripture quotations marked (NIV) are taken from the Holy Bible, New International Version®. NIV®. Copyright © 1973, 1978, 1984 by Biblica Inc.™ Used by permission of Zondervan. All rights reserved worldwide. www.zondervan.com.

Details in some anecdotes and stories have been changed to protect the identities of the persons involved.

ISBN 978-0-307-72965-1
ISBN 978-0-307-72966-8 (electronic)

Copyright © 2011 by Alisa Harris

Cover design by Kelly L. Howard

All rights reserved. No part of this book may be reproduced or transmitted in any form or by any means, electronic or mechanical, including photocopying and recording, or by any information storage and retrieval system, without permission in writing from the publisher.

Published in the United States by WaterBrook Multnomah, an imprint of the Crown Publishing Group, a division of Random House Inc., New York.

WATERBROOK and its deer colophon are registered trademarks of Random House Inc.

Library of Congress Cataloging-in-Publication Data
Harris, Alisa.
    Raised right : how I untangled my faith from politics / Alisa Harris. — 1st ed.
       p. cm.
    Includes bibliographical references (p.   ).
    ISBN 978-0-307-72965-1 — ISBN 978-0-307-72966-8
   1. Harris, Alisa. 2. Evangelicalism—United States. 3. Christianity and politics—United States. 4. Christian biography—United States. I. Title.
    BR1643.H27A3 2011
    277.3'083092—dc23
    [B]
                                                2011029147

Printed in the United States of America
2011—First Edition

10 9 8 7 6 5 4 3 2 1

SPECIAL SALES
Most WaterBrook Multnomah books are available at special quantity discounts when purchased in bulk by corporations, organizations, and special-interest groups. Custom imprinting or excerpting can also be done to fit special needs. For information, please e-mail SpecialMarkets@WaterBrookMultnomah.com or call 1-800-603-7051.

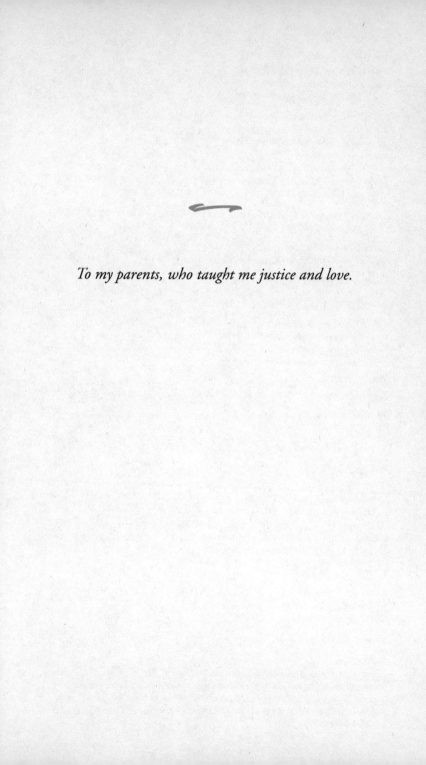

To my parents, who taught me justice and love.

CONTENTS

A Firmer Foundation

*I*n 1997 I was the picture of bold countercultural style. I wore my hair in a french braid dangling over an outré homemade green gingham jumper and was hanging out in the goat barn at the San Juan County Fair when the announcer said, "And we have a special guest this evening!" I looked over and saw one of my heroes, the man whose leadership I thought would bring America to its knees again: Bill Redmond, candidate for US representative. Dizzy with worship and seized with a boldness that came over me only when I was rallying for a political cause, I dragged my sister to his side and wedged us next in line. He cocked his head to the side, took my hand in his, and replied to my sputtering with a kind "Well, thank you so much." He had a pastor's trick of making it sound like a postsermon "Well, bless your heart. Praise the Lord for that."

Once, I heard him speak to a group of Christian teens at the state capitol. Just as a pastor would take a text from a book of the Bible, he announced, "Today we're going to look at the most important phrase in the most important sentence in the most important document in American history: the Declaration of Independence." This key phrase was "endowed by their Creator," he explained. If God, not government, gives rights, then government has no authority to take rights away—but if we didn't stand up and fight for our God-given rights, government *would* take them away. And if we didn't keep God in the public sphere, the basis for understanding inalienable rights would crumble.

He expounded in that distinct pastoral intonation, every consonant crisp, with three tidy main points, impeccable transitions, and a peroration that applied the Word to your own life. As he painted a picture of the stakes should we lose this election, my heart was clutched by the fear that others felt when they heard sermons of damnation and hell. I saw a future where we crept forth in the dead of night to worship God in the dark like the Pilgrims did in England and the Christians did in Soviet Russia. This was why we fought. This was why we voted and campaigned and knocked on doors.

So when Redmond ran for office again and faced a Republican-primary challenger who had less fervor for America's history as a Christian nation, I was ready to fight for the man who knew God was the source of America's greatness.

I arose early on a Saturday morning to learn the inner workings of the Republican machine and how to sanctify it for God's cause. My dad and I climbed into a private plane piloted by another Republican and took off for the GOP state convention. I looked out the tiny window and watched the golden land recede beneath us as we floated into the clouds. The roar of the engine shut out the conversation in the front, and I sat in the back floating off in my own world, remembering all Redmond had said about the stakes of this election and how any election could turn the tide of the world for good or ill. Just as one bad man could push America to ruin, one man anointed by God and in God's proper timing could turn the world upside down and then set it aright. Revival could bring revolution, and who better than a pastor turned politician to bring both at once?

Shortly after our plane landed, we entered the convention center, where candidates set up booths and distributed anything to which they could affix a campaign sticker. I wandered, collecting campaign paraphernalia for candidates I liked, conscientiously refusing buttons from moderates I despised, and drinking water from a bottle covered with campaign stickers for Redmond.

When it came time to vote for the candidate whose name would be first on the ballot, the county chairman—who was technically not allowed to take sides in primary elections but had not been called by God to a party leadership role to let liberal Republicans win primaries—gathered up the ballots for absentee voters and handed them all to me. I was too young to vote, but I checked off Bill Redmond's name on each one and stuffed the ballot box. "The pastors can preach," the county chair was fond of saying, "but they should leave the political machinations to me. I can get my hands dirty for God."

A few weeks earlier my family had gone to White Sands, New Mexico, a desert where scientists tested the atomic bomb. While the rest of the kids rolled in the glittering sand, I tore myself from my biography of Ronald Reagan long enough to trot across the sand and spell out a political campaign message: "REDMOND." There was no one for miles, and the wind would blow it away, but still I shuffled through the sand, spelling R-E-D-M... with my footsteps. I'm not sure who the message was for, since no one would see it but God.

FOR NEARLY ALL MY CHILDHOOD and adolescence, on into early adulthood, politics gave my faith meaning. Politics expressed my faith. Politics was my way of fighting for "a future and a hope,"[1] my way of proving I believed what Jesus said: "Take heart! I have overcome the world."[2] A surge of political fervor marked my soul's revival, and the vision of a godly America was my promised land. My faith was so intertwined with conservative politics that I viewed them as one and the same. In my ironclad worldview, faith and politics were inseparable.

So when I ventured out into the complicated world and found it shaking my confidence in the goodness of culture-war politics, my faith shook too. With the conservative political accoutrements of my evangelical Christianity stripped away, little of my faith remained.

This book was born out of my search for a faith that's more than the sum of my political convictions and for a meaningful way of living it out.

WHEN IT COMES TO POLITICS, the children of old-school evangelicals are undergoing a shift. We have yet to convince our parents that we are not rejecting what they taught us but living it out in a different way. My parents taught me to be suspicious of power, so when I see power concentrated in big corporations, big government, and big money, I become suspicious. My parents taught me to fight for the disenfranchised and weak—the child who couldn't pray in school or the businessman who couldn't work without government bullying. Today I feel compelled to combat injustice when I look at families torn apart by harsh immigration laws and when I see men wearing three-thousand-dollar suits while orchestrating the crash of the American economy. I hear a dad talk fondly of the American Dream as he enters a lottery to get his son into a decent school, and it outrages me that his son's fate rests on a gamble. My parents' hearts broke over the ugliness they saw in abortion clinics, and I am heartsick over the ugliness of wars in Iraq and elsewhere. But the lesson they taught me remains: when you see injustice, you have to speak up.

When I mention I'm writing a memoir about leaving the culture wars behind, people's first question is, "Aren't you young to be writing a memoir?" This is a delicate way of saying, *What can you possibly have to say? And what if you change your mind once you actually know what you're talking about?* Sometimes I think they're right. But most of the time, I think that I have no choice but to write this—for myself, for my peers, and for anyone interested in understanding us.

Yes, this book is for me. Writing is not just how I communicate my thoughts but how I actually think. It's the way an experience or a fleeting thought becomes real to me instead of floating away. It's the way I catch my thoughts and turn them over and over, testing their weight and deciding whether to keep them or throw them away. For me, to write is to become, and I can't become that older, wiser person without skewering these youthful thoughts to paper, without holding them up for my scrutiny and yours. The first drafts of this book illuminated my own failure to love. Working to correct those first bad drafts has made me strive for more charity in my everyday life. It has shown me that I don't always live out the things I know to be true because complaining about falsehood is so much more convenient than living out a radical alternative.

I am also writing this book for other ex–culture warriors who, like me, grew up with signs in their fists and are trying to figure out what to do with their now-empty hands. Like me, they were raised to be activists, and like me, they probably have felt lost as their belief in the nobility of the culture wars fades away. They are looking for some worthy cause where they can channel the passion for justice and truth, bestowed by their parents, into something that actually builds people's lives instead of tearing apart relationships and destroying faith.

Some of these young Christians know what they believe. Some don't. Some have fully embraced left-wing politics; some have just decided they are no longer Republicans. Some are trying to change their chosen political party from the inside, while others remain skeptical of the entire spectrum. But all of them recognize that something is deeply wrong with the evangelical politics in which our childhoods were immersed. Today, half of young churchgoers say Christians are "too involved in politics."[3] Almost half of young born-again Christians think the "political efforts of conservative Christians"[4] are a problem facing America. Less than half of young evangelicals identify as conservatives, compared to nearly two-thirds of their parents.[5] Fewer and fewer identify with the Republican Party. Where do we fit?

I hope this book reassures these young Christians that they are not alone as they navigate these difficult waters where the currents of faith and culture collide. I hope it helps them to remember that what our parents taught us about the importance of standing for truth remains valid. Perhaps their understanding of truth was wrong or incomplete. Perhaps their frenzied application of it was fruitless. But we cannot fault their passionate pursuit.

I'm also writing this for people who want to make sense of this strange new breed of Christian. Politicians are fumbling to connect with this growing segment of the population, trying to find what moves them to act. You can see it in Barack Obama's pointed outreach to the young evangelical vote—in the biblically redolent title he picked for his youth outreach, pitched so perfectly to the evangelical soul that a conservative Christian group immediately accused him of stealing it from them. Activist authors like Jim Wallis and Shane Claiborne are trying to recruit young Christians to their causes. Organizers are trying to mobilize them. Journalists are trying to understand them. You can see it in the spate of fawning articles that trot around phrases like "young evangelical" and "broadening evangelical agenda" and "increasing

passion for poverty and social justice." So often in these articles and focus groups and books, the ex-culture warriors are
presented as experimental subjects or generalized as a group.
But rarely are they given a voice, beyond the punchy sound
bite, that explains how they got to where they are today.

Our parents are the ones most earnestly trying to make
sense of it all. My own mother is sympathetic but does not
understand. She said she never expected to have a child who
became Catholic, as my sister has done, nor one who voted
Democrat, as I have done. She thinks if that's the worst we
ever do, then she has little reason to complain. But still, why
the change? I hope this book will help her and others to
understand that this change is not a rejection of the core
truths they've passed on to us but a different application of
them. Our actions and beliefs are an expansion of the principles of justice and love that they imparted, not a rejection
of those principles.

This book is not a liberal credo or a political platform; in
fact, this book is born of a struggle to find a faith that tran-
scends credos and platforms. It is a halting, flawed attempt
to hew a faith that is more solid and graspable than the slogans I once traced in sand.

Flesh and Blood

I marched down the side of a highway, clutching a sign in my fist. My baby sister bounced in the carrier on my mother's back, while her left hand gripped my sister and her right hand held a sign. My dad led the way with my three-year-old brother on his shoulders and his own sign held in front of him. I lifted my sign as high as I could.

Cars blew past as people put their heads out the windows and screamed "Go to hell!" and "Separation of church and state!" They honked their horns and stuck their fists out the windows, raising their middle fingers in salute.

"Why are they doing that?" I asked my mom while mimicking the gesture.

"Don't do that, honey. It's not a very nice thing. They're just not being nice."

The Oregon sun seared my head, and my feet ached from thumping against the hot pavement, but we kept marching, indifferent to jeers. The woman behind me started asking God to bind the forces of darkness and cast out the demons who sat on young women's shoulders and urged them to murder their babies. The people around her took up the murmur. Soon the line of marchers was murmuring, "Amen," and as the woman reached a crescendo, they said, "Thank You, Jesus."

A car drove past. The driver rolled down his window and made the not-nice gesture while his twenty-something passenger rolled down her back window and gave us the thumbs-up—a gesture of derision from the front seat and a gesture of support from the back.

I didn't understand why we were here, where we were trying to go, and why we had to care so much that we trudged so long. I was too young to know we were fighting a war, but I was a child soldier on the front lines.

I HAD BEEN PICKETING since before I could walk. Before my parents moved to Oregon from New Mexico, they had bundled me into a carrier twice a week and hauled me and their signs to the local abortion clinic, where they paced the road across the street, praying as pregnant women walked in and empty women came out. They preached the pro-life message to churches and pastors, building contacts and a network of people who could mobilize activists quickly. My father could rattle off Supreme Court cases and grisly facts in church presentations, while my mother told the pastors the story of her own abortion long ago and her lingering regret.

When the local hospital bought the building where the doctors performed abortions, my father, who worked ten-hour days in the mud of the oil field, changed from his Levi's into a suit and went to meet with the hospital administrators. Not above some good old-fashioned political pressure, he explained that he and his group would continue to picket the clinic twice a week if the hospital kept performing abortions. They would also take their own wives, who would give birth to several more children than the American average, all the way to a hospital in another state. He gave the administrators the pro-life newsletter he helped compile and explained it had a mailing list three hundred citizens long: three hundred citizens, in a tiny community, who would know and care that San Juan Regional Medical Center owned a clinic where doctors killed babies. Plenty of people to take picketing shifts.

The next time he met with the hospital administrators, they said they were relieving the offending doctors of their duties. "We don't do abortions in San Juan County," an administrator said. And from that day on, they didn't.

When we read Old Testament passages like the story of Rahab and I asked my mom what a prostitute was, she said, "Women that men paid to act like their wives," which conjured confusing pictures of paid cooks and housekeepers. When I asked how the single mom in our church had a baby without a husband, she said the mom "acted like she was married." Apparently I was too young to know how people made babies but not too young to know how they killed them. Once, at one of my parents' pro-life action meetings, I left the children with their tedious games and went to see what the adults were doing. I crept into the room at the moment an image of a dead baby, swollen with blood and thrown on a trash heap, flashed onto the screen. The image would continue to haunt me whenever I saw pictures of unborn babies floating—fragile, with veins lacing their eyelids, their tiny toes curled and their thumbs in their mouths—in clouds that looked like jellyfish frills in the sea.

At home we had two tiny pink plastic embryos that bounced from room to room. Once used at the crisis-pregnancy center my parents helped start to encourage women to "choose life," the babies now rattled around with the Legos and Lincoln Logs. We played with them as we would with born babies, since they looked like tiny babies crouched into balls. The fingernail-sized gold pin that my mother fastened to her fifth child's diaper bag showed two feet with ten perfect toes about a quarter-inch tall, the exact size of an unborn baby's feet at ten weeks' gestation. Even a child like me could see they were a baby's feet and not a blob of tissue.

Growing up in pro-life circles, I heard people give the exhortation, "Deliver those who are drawn toward death, and hold back those stumbling to the slaughter."[1] They said, "A voice is heard in Ramah, mourning and great weeping, Rachel weeping for her children and refusing to be comforted, because her children are no more."[2] My aunt was an obstetrician, and if she had performed abortions, my father said they would have paced her sidewalk too, holding signs: "Abortion stops a beating heart" and "Unborn babies are people too."

I stood at another rally years later, this time as a journalist instead of a protester. A bill legalizing gay marriage had just smoothly passed the New York State Assembly and was waiting for approval in the Senate. Thousands of people, bused in by Hispanic clergy to protest, pressed behind barricades the New York Police Department had positioned in front of the Manhattan office of David Paterson, the governor. NYPD cops—exuding that impassive, genial objectivity I also strove for—expanded the barricades again and again to let more people in. The crowd throbbed to a Dominican beat, lifted Bibles, and raised signs that read *"Un hombre + una mujer = Voluntad de Dios."* One man and one woman equals God's will.

The pastors mounted the platform and bellowed Leviticus 18, with all its bald, blunt commands: "Do not lie with a man as one lies with a woman; that is detestable."[3] They quoted Romans 1: "For this cause God gave them up unto vile affections: for even their women did change the natural use into that which is against nature: And likewise also the men, leaving the natural use of the woman, burned in their lust one toward another; men with men working that which is unseemly, and receiving in themselves that recompence of their error which was meet."[4] A pastor turned state senator read the names of Hispanic assemblymen who had voted for gay marriage while the crowd booed after each name. A Jewish leader pointed to the size of the crowd and rejoiced, "There are many more God-fearing citizens in this state than there are deviants and perversions." Despite this assertion of such a "moral majority," he painted a picture in which all Christian freedom would disappear, yelling, "Where will we go when the state says we're bigots? Who will take us out of jail?… If, God forbid, you pass this legislation, next year the perverts will come to you: We demand that uncles can marry nephews. We demand that nephews can marry aunts, and this will also be taught in the schools. You are making this into Sodom on the Hudson." And hearkening to that picture of destruction, he shouted, "We pray to You, God—do not punish us because of the evil and wicked ones."

Detestable. Vile. Against nature. Perverts.

Then the pastors roared prayers to the heavens, prefacing their rebukes to Governor Paterson with, "Oh, almighty God!" No one in the crowd bowed their heads or stretched their arms; they cheered and booed as the prayers required. One pastor shouted, "The noise that we make is not political; it's worshiping the God of heaven." Then he prayed for mercy on Governor Paterson, saying he was "doubly blind: physically blind, spiritually blind." They called on Paterson to use his political power to reform immigration instead.

As the crowd yelled, I would at times forget that these were supposed to be prayers until I would catch an "Almighty God!" or "Lord, we pray!" Then I'd unbow my head from my scribbling and remember that I was hearing words directed at God but intended for the people filling the streets—these pastors, these protesters, and especially those cameras right over there. Their efforts projected the same deafening roar I'd heard in prayers before, where people seem to be shouting so loud that no one could possibly hear God's response to their pleas. I couldn't help but think of the kind of ostentatious prayers Jesus chided: "And when you pray, do not be like the hypocrites, for they love to pray standing in the synagogues and on the street corners to be seen by men."[5] He must have meant, *Pray to Me and not to the cameras. When you pray, talk to Me.*

On my way to the heart of the protest, I had followed the crowds threading through the barricades and passed a modest counterprotest. The real, much larger counterprotest took place in another part of the city, where city council members, the mayor, and the gay senator who'd sponsored the bill were making speeches. Just a few people came here for appearances' sake, doing their best to throw the others into bigoted relief with a beatific display of forgiveness.

They lifted signs that said "Thank you, Governor" and "Marriage is so gay." They chanted, "Hate is a sin!"

The Christians screamed back, "We don't hate you!"

The gays: "Yes, you do, and you're probably gay!"

"Adam and Eve!"

"God created Adam and Eve. Then He created Adam and Steve."

And a gay, not a Christian: "God bless you!"

"We're just trying to get our voices heard, that society is trying to promote perversion as normal," a Christian protester told me. "God loves the homosexuals. He loves the lesbians. He doesn't love the sin." Another protester told me, "True Christians do not hate anyone."

If this was love, why did it sound like a curse?

I left the protest and took the train to Brooklyn to have brunch at a friend's house, watching the graffiti-covered concrete hurtle past the windows and thinking about the scene I'd left behind. Jesus said they would know us by our love, and love was the stated reason for all these signs and picket lines; the sign wavers believed they were protecting homosexuals from their self-destructive sin and helping them find a better way. Perhaps they believed their rebukes communicated love, just as a caring parent rebukes a child. That the child sees the chastising as cruel doesn't change the fact that the parent has the child's best interests at heart.

Then I realized why these efforts at love sounded hollow—because this love was not the way I experienced love every day. Even setting aside the arrogance suggested by viewing all other sinners as children and saved sinners as the world's *in loco parentis,* I know my parents love me because they sacrificed to feed and clothe me every day. In the end that burden of labor and sacrifice is what gives them any right to be heard or believed when they say "I love you" after they say "You're wrong."

That scripture my parents taught me—about delivering those who are going to death and holding back those who are stumbling to slaughter—held a different meaning for me now. The image in my mind was one of physical sacrifice, of throwing one's entire body into the rescue with no regard for self. Carrying a sign seemed a cowardly kind of love, one that isolated you behind a barricade, futilely shouting at the world while it stumbled past. I was looking for a more incarnational love, and while I couldn't define it in so many words, I knew it when I saw it.

ON ANOTHER ASSIGNMENT I traveled deep into the belly of Queens, where I knocked on the door of a tiny house. A stooped elderly woman greeted me, and I squeezed into a kitchen piled high with coolers and pans of rice, meat stew, pasta, and vegetables. I followed her single file through a narrow aisle that led to her bedroom off the kitchen. Murmuring apologies that she spoke no English, she gestured for me to sit down on the bed, then took a folding chair and knotted her arthritic hands in her lap. Her grandson—a bright-eyed little boy of five—took over the conversation and asked where I worked, if I wanted to watch television, if I wanted to play catch. We tossed a ball back and forth in the living room as we waited for his mother and uncle to come home.

Meanwhile the grandmother moved her folding chair to the kitchen and supervised a younger woman and a quiet young man as they dished the food—a little meat, a little rice, a bagel—into foam containers and neatly packed them in the coolers. They moved deliberately, as if they were cooking a family dinner for one hundred people, with none of the rush I'd seen at other mass dinners.

By the time Jorge Muñoz arrived, three hours after I did,

I felt like the day should be over. But for the bus driver who has commandeered his mother's home for a soup kitchen, it was just beginning. We sat in the living room on an old car seat that doubled as a couch.

Jorge, a short man whose hands have been roughened with labor, said he feels sorry for his mom, her house filled up with boxes of food and her kitchen full of people cooking all day. "It's not a house anymore—it's a storage! Look at this," he said and laughed, gesturing to the boxes of oatmeal and bags of rice stacked everywhere. He said, "She's happy," despite the boxes of Frosted Flakes piled high in her living room.

Four years earlier Jorge had been waiting in his school bus to pick up a load of kids from summer camp when he saw two camp employees throwing away aluminum pans full of leftover food. Appalled at the waste, he asked why, and they said they had to throw out leftover food every day. He asked for the food so he could give it away. He passed it along to a needy family at his church at first, but then he noticed day laborers standing on corners waiting for work.

"Then one night I saw one of those guys who was standing there in the day, standing there at the night. I asked him, 'What are you guys doing here?'"

Waiting for the police to leave so they could creep under the bridge to sleep, the men said.

"Have you eaten?" he asked.

"We don't work, we don't eat."

He told them to wait, and he would bring them food.

He fed eight men under the bridge each night the first week, twenty-four men the second week. Forty men came each night for the rest of the first year and more each year after that. When Jorge lost his job and was unemployed for six weeks, he prayed for food and kept feeding them. Once, a boy from Jorge's home country, Colombia, sold brownies and iced coffee to send Jorge a twenty-five-dollar donation; and once, a man Jorge had fed came back after he found a job and a home and gave Jorge twenty dollars to thank him for his care. "Things like that make me be moved to do more and more. God is the One who supports me.... You ask how I started and how I keep doing this. It's God."

Hidalgo, the quiet young man in the kitchen packing up food, had stood in Jorge's line and slept on the street for nine months until someone lobbed a beer bottle at him, slicing his face. The boy was afraid to go to the doctor and hadn't showered in two weeks, so Jorge took him in, and his mother treated Hidalgo like another son.

Jorge and Hidalgo packed the coolers into a pickup

truck, and I climbed in the front seat next to Jorge. We drove through the dark night and bright lights of Queens, stopping by a local bakery to pick up some leftover bread as the employees turned the chairs upside down on the tables and swept the empty shop. Then we drove on and made our second stop at his church, where he picked up three volunteers. Jorge bustled around, shuffling crates of food until he could wedge them into the backseat. I turned around and tried to make conversation, but they smiled the same polite, apologetic smiles of Jorge's mother. No English spoken here either.

As we drove on, Jorge told me that one night when it was ten degrees, he saw twenty-three men sleeping under the bridge. He clicked his tongue: "That's a lot." Once, two of the men snoozed under the bridge after sunup, and they awoke soaked in gasoline, their flesh on fire. Jorge doctored one man with antibiotics and painkillers to deaden the pain in his scarred right arm and face; the other man disappeared.

By the time we drove up to the bridge, a group of men waited silently in the pools of rain and sodden refuse. Jorge hopped out, tied a garbage bag around a fire hydrant to collect the trash, and threw open the coolers, spearing a plastic fork into the top of each foam container before he passed it to a man in line. A helper stood in the truck bed and handed out loaves of bread from white grocery bags. The men squatted in the rain with their backs against a brick wall and ate.

I asked Jorge if he got tired of waking up at five in the morning, working all day, then coming home and doing all this. "Sometimes I get home around five, five thirty, a little bit tired, but every time I get tired, I put myself in that position," he said. "I just put my energies and—okay, let's go. They waiting. They gonna be waiting for food."

As I walked away and climbed the slippery stairs to the subway platform, Jorge was still breaking loaves of bread in the rain.

UNLESS YOU ARE SMUGGLING SOUP to the Jews in your attic, I think a political act can't be an act of love. It can be a good act, even noble and heroic, but love is not something that takes place behind a barricade; it happens in the breaking of bread and the passing of cups. Political love is theoretical, directed at some vague "humanity," and Jesus didn't say to love humanity but to love your neighbor. A quote from Dostoevsky's *The Brothers Karamazov* comes back to me. "In my dreams," an older man tells a younger, "I have often come to making enthusiastic schemes for the service of humanity, and perhaps I might actually have faced crucifixion if it had been suddenly necessary; and yet I am incapable of living in the same room with any one for two days together.... But it has always happened that the more I detest men individually the more ardent becomes my love for humanity."[6]

I am like that old man. The more ardently I see humanity as a glorious abstract that must conform to my ideal of how the world should be, the harder it is for me to love the person on the other side of the picket line who is holding up progress. I can love the downtrodden in abstract, but as I shivered under the bridge that night with Jorge, I realized that it's harder to love the illegal immigrant with the bottle-slashed face and the body unwashed for weeks, the workers gathering to eat day-old bread and chicken and rice out of foam containers, the crowd of thousands clamoring for bread and fish and healing, the unclean woman hoping to touch the hem of the Savior's robe. Dostoevsky also said, "Love in action is a harsh and dreadful thing compared with love in dreams. Love in dreams is greedy for immediate action, rapidly performed and in the sight of all.... But active love is labour and fortitude."[7]

Physical involvement is implicit in the command "Hold

back those stumbling to the slaughter."[8] It commands bodily sacrifice—labor—that goes beyond the holding of a sign or the giving of a speech. It commands us to be not bystanders but participants in a dangerous world. Love in dreams is fatigued by its neighbor's needs for food and safety. Love in action works for the unwashed and hungry people who are waiting in the pools of rain and soggy trash. The world as a whole may not change, but our neighbor's world, and by extension ours, grows brighter—even when breaking loaves of bread in the rain.

2

On Earth as It Is in Heaven

*A*cowboy rides up to a saloon and ties his horse to a post, then parts his coat to reveal a pearl-handled gun with a blue blaze of light whipping around it. Spurs clanking, he stalks into the saloon and shoots up the hellish gang carousing inside. He crushes the skull of the Demon of Alcoholism by cracking him over the head with his own bottle of liquor. He punches a deformed dwarf, then takes a mandolin and bashes it over the head of the Demon of

False Religion. Then he curls his lip in a holy snarl and calls on his real prey—the leader of the hellish crew—to come forth.

Powerless to resist his own demise, the leader, a straggly blond with vampiric incisors, strides onto the scene with a bravado that fails to cloak his fear. He struggles to yank his gun out of his holster, but it seems glued down. The cowboy loads his bullets and blows two glowing holes in the Devil, who falls backward out of the saloon's swinging doors. As the cowboy's crippled enemy trembles in the dust, the cowboy jeers, "Well, how do you feel about that, Devil?"

"I'm afeelin' mighty low."

"Good."

The music video on the screen at the front of our church reminded me that we were fighting a war. Carman, the Christian pop music artist turned cowboy, reminded me. Our youth group reminded me when they reenacted Carman's song to great acclaim, carousing on the church stage with bottles of apple juice while the pastor's son strode between the church pews wearing a black hat and boots and chanting, "Satan: bite the dust."

I'd been reminded regularly since my preschool days in children's church, where I marched in place and bobbed up and down, spreading my arms into plane wings while I sang,

I may never march with the infantry,
>ride in the cavalry,
>shoot the artillery.
I may never fly o'er the enemy.
But I'm in the Lord's Army.
Yes sir!

I may not have been clear on the pronunciation, let alone definition, of *cavalry,* but I knew what it meant to be in the Lord's Army—that Satan hated me for my power over him, that he and his minions warred against me with the weapons of sickness, despair, and idolatry. I'd heard my pastor pace the stage and bellow the words of Paul: "For we wrestle not against flesh and blood, but against principalities, against powers, against the rulers of the darkness of this world, against spiritual wickedness in high places."[1] Our champion in this fight: the Holy Spirit.

I had seen the Spirit move when people held hands in a circle and interspersed their prayer with strange languages I couldn't understand, but I witnessed it mightily just once. While Pastor John was speaking, one of my parents' friends, Greg, came forward and lifted his hands to ask for prayer. Pastor John reached out his hand and shouted, "I bind you, Satan, in the name of Jesus Christ!" The moment he said,

"Jesus Christ," Greg staggered as if shot through the heart and then fell flat on his back, lying spread-eagled on the floor with a smile on his face. Later he marveled, "It was like Someone was just pushing against my chest, pinning me to the floor and saying, 'Don't get up. Don't get up.'" A shiver passed through my body at the realization that some unseen power could pin you to the floor like a bug.

Despite the spiritual warfare waged all around me, I never felt the darkness. The devil lurked in every shadow, but my childhood was a sunlit merry-go-round of happy home and church—no indifferent teachers, no bullies since my mother taught me at home. I looked for times when I could rebuke the devil so I could feel a surge of power rushing out like Jesus did when the bleeding woman touched His robe and was healed—but no opportunities came. Other children went to sleep and dreamed of heaven, standing up and sharing their visions with the rest of the class on Sunday, but I never had these dreams. Never spoke in tongues. Never felt that force of the Holy Spirit entering me or His magic shooting out.

Others sensed the Enemy always present, when a cold breath of air prickled the skin on their necks, when they were praying and felt so full of the Spirit that they knew the Enemy was lurking for attack. And yet we had no need to

fear. The forces of darkness—Demons of Negativity, Demons of Alcoholism, Demons of Depression, of Disbelief, of
Divorce, of Sickness, of Strife, of Poverty, and most of all the
Demons of Fear—could be easily vanquished by anyone
with faith the size of the mustard seed my mother kept in a
pendant. As Pastor John reminded us, "God has not given us
a spirit of fear, but of power and of love and of a sound
mind."[2]

Since our shields of faith deflected all the fiery darts of
the Evil One,[3] church felt like both a battle and a celebration.
We were at war, but we enacted scenes that felt more like a
pep rally, with all of us waving flags and skipping in place at
the front of the church, as cheerleaders for Jesus Christ.

Everything was splashed with color and light and music.
My dad led worship services—one song after the other with
no list, just playing the next song and repeating the chorus as
the Holy Ghost led. Banners draped from poles reached almost to the balcony above—strips of sparkling fabric sewn
together, lettered with the names of God in gold: *Elohim, El
Shaddai, Adonai*. When the Spirit moved, people would lift
the banners from their stands and march them, billowing,
down the aisle of the church while we all followed in dance.
I wore a silky white gown with a row of lace at the bottom
and put on a sash of smooth fabric that my Sunday-school

teacher said represented my tribe of Israel—Dan. In front of the church, I danced, waving an iridescent flag while the woman next to me banged a tambourine in time.

Once, we marched around our stone church seven times to commemorate the seven times the Israelites marched around Jericho. On the seventh time, Pastor John raised the shofar, a twisted ram's horn, to his lips and blew a terrible blast that would shatter the walls of darkness.

It was a victory rally, because we had already won the war.

BUT SUCH BREEZY CONFIDENCE was a mistake, my parents said. So many thought their work was done—and yet unborn babies were dying and the world was slipping into hell, into the same wretched destiny my parents had only narrowly escaped.

My father was the son of two alcoholics, the grandson of another. The first time he tasted alcohol at age thirteen, he got so drunk he had to hold the walls to stay upright. From then on he couldn't stop, going on binges where he was so crazy for booze that he would bash in a liquor-store window to get it. He was scoring dope in Central Park. He was stumbling drunk and getting mugged in the Meatpacking District. He was in jail. He was in detox, shaking with the d.t.'s. He was going to Alcoholics Anonymous meetings twice a day to ward off addiction, and he was praying obsessively— *God, grant me the serenity to accept the things I cannot change; God, grant me the serenity*—to stop his body from shaking when he was racked with anxiety attacks.

Then he and a woman he'd met in AA were facing an unplanned pregnancy. He took refuge in the idea that it was a woman's choice, not his responsibility to decide—until she went to the local crisis-pregnancy center and came back with pictures of an unborn baby. After one look at the baby floating and sucking her thumb, he said there was no question. They wouldn't have an abortion. He married the woman.

All too soon he was getting divorced and trying to stay dad to three kids. Two years later he was falling in love with my mom. Then he was holding my skinny white baby body in his big brown hands, and he was promising himself that my life would be different, that I would have the education and the spiritual guidance he lacked, that I would know God and know truth and do the things he could have done if he'd been given the chance.

My mother was the daughter of a psychologist and a nutritionist, the third of five children plus one her mother

aborted because she hadn't even wanted five. Raised an athe-
ist, she became a Catholic, then Catholic Charismatic, then
just plain Charismatic. She taught Navajo kids on the New
Mexico reservation—kids who had no place to go when she
dismissed her class at the end of the day. She was thinking
she might never marry and might become a missionary,
when one day she sat next to my dad on a bus trip to church
camp. Not too long afterward she was married, and on
Election Day 1984, she lay in the hospital counting my fingers and toes while my dad went to the polls and cast his vote
to reelect Ronald Reagan. She promised herself that I would
know God and know truth and not carry the sorrow that
used to weigh on her so heavily.

My parents knew firsthand that the Enemy was still at
war, claiming lives just as he had tried to claim theirs. Yet all
the other parents in our church were so dreamily intent on
Jesus's returning soon that they failed to notice the groaning
earth in front of them. They sent their children into the combat zone of public school, where they learned to do drugs and
make babies. They shrugged off politics as inconsequential,
because evil would wax worse and worse before Jesus returned and there was nothing we could do to stop it. They
thought we should welcome the wickedness as a sign of the
end times, a reminder of the imminent day when Jesus would

take us up in an instant to a world where there was no more crying or pain or sadness, where the lion would lie down with the lamb and a little child would lead them.[4] Jesus was coming soon, perhaps before their children grew into adulthood, so why work to make the world a better place?

My parents moved the family to Oregon for nine months to clear their minds and get a fresh perspective. When we came back, we started attending another church where no one anointed people with olive oil and the sermon lasted the prescribed twenty minutes instead of as long as the Spirit led.

As my parents extricated themselves from our old church, I started to grasp another kind of war, one that took place on earth and among flesh and blood. While I rode with my dad to the grocery store in his battered blue Datsun pickup truck, Rush Limbaugh's voice boomed through the radio talking about the feminazis and the Communist News Network. Dittoheads called in, angry about environmentalist wackos and leftists. During commercials my dad turned down the radio and talked to me about the need to have a Christian kind of politics that was somehow the same as Rush Limbaugh's. My history textbook told me that God's hand was on America from its founding and that just as He chose David to save Israel and Jonathan to save David, He chose John Smith to save Jamestown, Pocahontas to save John

Smith, the Pilgrims to save the Indians, Squanto to save the Pilgrims, and the Founders to save America and create a nation that would become God's new chosen people—the "new Israel."

This new Israel held the future of Christianity. God intended it to be the light of the world, the city on a hill. Though I wouldn't have put it in these words at the time, I came to believe that our battle was not against invisible demons but against evil people who brought the fight into the real world. They were the spiritual enemy clothed in flesh: abortionists, feminists, secularists, humanists, the people conspiring to destroy God's witness by corrupting America. Finally I had an enemy I could see and point out to others, one that didn't require a mysterious intuition or the spiritual gift of discernment to identify. This fight made more sense because I had never actually felt the prickle of the Evil Demon or the physical warmth of the Holy Ghost. I'd found it too hard to conjure up a vision of the enemy. Now it was easy: the faces I saw on television at my grandmother's house, the pictures in the newspaper.

I began to see a vision of heaven on earth where justice prevailed and everyone followed God's rules—a vision we could accomplish through politics by out-arguing, out-picketing, and out-voting our enemies. America's current decadence was just a forty-year blip in its history of fearing God and following Him, so I could join Rush Limbaugh and help turn back the clock to make it into a God-fearing nation once again. Sin and evil were still outside of me instead of in me, and Jesus was not Someone who gave victory over the sin in myself but a shadowy figure who had left us to work for the salvation of the world through politics. Because I was on the right side, victory would come as easily as bopping a villain over the head with a cardboard mandolin.

By electing the right people and defeating Satan's human emissaries, we could usher in heaven on earth.

IN EARLY CHILDHOOD I HAD WAGED spiritual war with little thought of earth, and as a teen I threw myself into political war with little thought of heaven. I find that now I struggle to live with the tension between the earthly darkness and the heavenly promise, knowing that the world's suffering is not as easily vanquished as I once thought it could be—by a quick rebuke or a suave politician. But the battle will come to an end, the meek will have justice, and Christ will judge the poor with righteousness.

Although my politics have shifted, one constant has remained: the temptation to believe that each political battle marks the beginning of God's kingdom or the end of the world, the start of heaven or beginning of hell. I find myself seething at all the people who just can't see the light the way I see it. This seething defines American politics on all sides. In *To Change the World: The Irony, Tragedy, and Possibility of Christianity in the Late Modern World,* James Davison Hunter argues that American politics, including the politics of the Christian Right and the Christian Left, is predicated on *ressentiment*—the belief that my enemies are committing a wave of atrocities against me, that I am a disenfranchised victim seeking the will to dominate my enemies because they are snatching the privileges I'm entitled to. When we operate from this perspective, every question—and every answer—is political.[5]

I can chart the *ressentiment* on both sides to a single day in June. At 9:00 a.m. I read a press release from the Catholic League, which expresses their outrage that the owners of the Empire State Building are refusing to light up the building in honor of Mother Teresa. They take it as an assault against a beleaguered minority, as yet another example of how the overlords of a godless city are out to crush them. They also comment on the recent release of a Lady Gaga video and how she "manages to get raped" in a video filled with Catholic imagery. They call her "the new poster girl for…Catholic bashing"—another enemy whose goal is to smash the church.

I read about a conservative attack on a tiny Internet publisher that includes a disclaimer at the end of its publications of the Constitution and the Declaration of Independence: "This book is a product of its time and does not reflect the same values as it would if it were written today. Parents might wish to discuss with their children how views on race, gender, sexuality, ethnicity, and interpersonal relations have changed since this book was written." The article quotes Amazon customers who describe the disclaimer as "insulting," "sickening," and "frankly, horrifying"—an assault on people who still hold the Founders' values dear. My research shows that the publisher also prints this disclaimer on *The Communist Manifesto*, *The Complete Works of Friedrich Nietzsche*, and *The Picture of Dorian Gray*. The words that conservatives viewed as an act of warfare targeted their opponents as well.

And in California, where judges' races are rarely political and almost never contested, a group of Christians were, with the help of the gun-owners' lobby, making things partisan. According to one candidate, "We believe our country is under assault and needs Christian values."[6] His answer was not to live out Christian values but to enforce them by seeking power.

And my own soul is not immune to anger and fear because, at the end of the day, I am seething too. I think that the Catholic League should take a look at the sexual violence its own church has concealed, and I sympathize with Lady Gaga's comment that she is "a quite religious woman that is very confused about religion."[7] I mentally label the Amazon reviewers as stupid and shrill in their response to a perceived attack, but my words carry some of that same shrillness. I believe my criticisms are valid, but I find they swallow my mind and warp my perspective until each slight becomes cataclysmic. Each dig at me—the *Communist Manifesto*–reading, Lady Gaga–listening, pacifist-leaning Christian—becomes another reason to assert my own will to dominate over my enemies. This *ressentiment* poisons a culture where everything—from the color of lights in a building to the disclaimers in the front of a book—has become a political battle. I struggle to let go of the drive to dominate and instead remember that heaven isn't forced on earth through my pursuit of power. We can't "change the world" like we want to, but one day it will change.

On the second Sunday of Advent, my husband and I

went to church at the Cathedral of Saint John the Divine in upper Manhattan. We sat in the straight-backed wooden chairs, wrapped in our coats to ward off the chilly air. The choir walked forward, with the children's voices high and heavenly, singing a slow song that welcomed the Redeemer's coming. They shook incense, and it clung to the air around me in a kind of anointing, reminding me of the way people in my childhood church touched a person's face with oil before they prayed for him. As the choristers sang, they traveled from the west to the east, symbolizing our own pilgrimage from darkness to light. The Scripture readings showed first the promise of God to those who walk in darkness and finally the fulfillment of the promise in the birth of Christ. After the choir climbed the steps to the altar, the reader ascended to the podium and read from Isaiah the promise to a people in darkness. His voice echoed off the stained glass and stone walls:

With righteousness He shall judge the poor,
And decide with equity for the meek of the earth....

The wolf also shall dwell with the lamb,
The leopard shall lie down with the young goat,

The calf and the young lion and the fatling together;
And a little child shall lead them.…

They shall not hurt nor destroy in all My holy
    mountain,
For the earth shall be full of the knowledge of
    the Lord
As the waters cover the sea.[8]

I found myself startled anew by the beauty of that passage and how my own preoccupations with policy minutiae fell far short of the vision God promised. Even if God were to make me tyrant of the world and give me power to reshape it as I see fit, even if I won every political battle I waged, I could never create the world that Christ will one day bring to the poor and meek. The most brazen campaign promises fall short of His.

The only way to defeat the politics of *ressentiment* is to remember that the kingdom of God is here but not yet realized: we still live in the earth's darkness, but we hold on to the heavenly promise. Instead of seeking power, I want to work for the kingdom's picture of peace. I want to be delivered from selfishness, find release from envy, and prepare for the day when "they shall not hurt nor destroy in all My holy mountain" by giving up my own power to hurt and destroy. And I want to remember that the world's redemption begins every day with a battle to recover hope and love in my own soul.

3

Of Goats and Sheep

I shifted from side to side, shaking sawdust from my high heels as I waited for the moment when I would enter the arena and make my stand. The crowd roared as the announcer spoke the name of the girl ahead of me and then the boy next to me. I whispered to myself the Teddy Roosevelt quote I lived by: "The credit belongs to the man who is actually in the arena, whose face is marred by dust and sweat and blood;...who knows the great enthusiasms, the great devotions; who spends himself in a worthy cause."[1] This was my moment. When the announcer said my name, I stepped into the sawdust ring, beamed at the audience, and gave a massive tug on the collar of the goat lunging behind me.

I was redeeming the San Juan County Fair Annual Goat Costume Contest for the cause of Christ.

Several years earlier my parents had moved their brood of six children to thirteen acres of green alfalfa grass and had, with the firm belief that doing things we did not want to do would build us into sturdy citizens of moral fiber, purchased two emotionally unstable goats we milked and fed twice a day. Each year we carted them to the San Juan County Fair and penned them up in the goat barn, next to the sleek creatures the real 4-H kids fostered. Our goats bleated angrily all day until we took them out and lugged them around a ring, where we always lost to the 4-H kids with their serious white jeans and beatific animals.

I endured the competition because free county-fair admission was one of the perks, and I loved to go to the country concerts and wander through the exhibits to find the prize jams and afghans of the people I knew. Midway through the week we came to the highlight: the Annual Goat Costume Contest, in which goat owners and their livestock donned costumes and mugged for the audience, whose applause level determined the prizewinner. I had played it safe in past years: Dorothy and Toto, Laura Ingalls

Wilder and her dog, Jack. But this year, as I reflected on that big captive audience, I realized they should be instructed in truth as well as entertained. The idea came so easily I knew it had to be sent from Somewhere.

I would be Hillary Clinton.

She and William Jefferson Clinton were among the figures I most loathed. Bill Clinton committed impeachable offenses as casually as other presidents played rounds of golf. I learned how to identify charlatans from listening to conservative analysis of his testimonies. *Was he moving his eyes to the left or the right, up or down? How many times did he touch his nose? How did you know Slick Willie was lying? He was moving his lips.* Hillary had as much as confessed to being his co-conspirator in all but adultery, since she had once declared, "If you vote for my husband, you get me; it's a two-for-one, blue-plate special." I could educate Middle America on this couple's nefarious ways by testifying at the San Juan County Fair Annual Goat Costume Contest that Hillary Clinton had, in a distinctly fascist way, ordered an underling to access the FBI files of her political enemies.

The night of the contest, I curled my hair to flip out at the bottom, then drenched it in hair spray so it wouldn't go limp in the sawdust-thick heat of the goat barn. I found two manila file folders, marked them "CONFIDENTIAL" in letters large enough that the audience could easily get the joke, coated my fingers with ink, and pressed them all over the file to represent Clinton's hands. I stepped into a blue thrift-store dress I'd purchased for the occasion—a matronly number about six sizes too big—then made myself a name tag and a sign that said "Two-for-one, blue-plate special." I hauled my goat, flailing, into a blue pantsuit and affixed a sign on her back: "Slick Willie." Dragging her out to the edge of the arena, I shoved us in line.

As I looked around at the competition—a teacher and student, an astronaut and an alien—I felt dizzy with glee at my creativity and my zeal to leave no witnessing opportunity unturned. I looked up at the audience in the green bleachers, eating their cotton candy, and prayed that tonight my confrontation would rescue that one person whose apathy would dissipate as the truth dawned: "Hillary Clinton really *is* a terrible person to steal confidential files!"

When the announcer called out, "Bill and Hillary Clinton," I strutted into the ring.

"Let's give it up for the Alien and the Astronaut!" the announcer urged. A girl wearing a headband with bouncing alien eyes waved her hand.

"Let's give it up for the Schoolteacher and the Student."

A girl dragged a goat wearing a dress with a chalkboard hanging around its neck. Wild cheers.

"And for Hillary and Bill Clinton!" I waved my file furiously and grinned. The cheers died down.

We didn't win, but winning—in a world you inherit when men revile you, persecute you, and say all matter of evil against you—was not the point. Like Socrates I was a gadfly—always provoking, stinging citizens out of complacency, and melodramatically drinking the hemlock they forced on me in punishment. I wore my costume and my name tag all night, even while we wandered through the exhibit hall, eating food samples and stopping by the county GOP booth to take their Tootsie Rolls and help them proselytize. As long as I wore it, the provocation went on and I felt powerful, like I was changing the world, one altercation at a time.

SINCE JESUS HAD DECLARED, "I did not come to bring peace but a sword,"[2] I believed my Christlike duty was to polarize, to separate the wheat from the chaff, the sheep from the goats, and the saved from the damned by charging every gathering with a controversy that forced people to take a stand and pick a side. I might have come to the goat contest as Pippi Longstocking and God would not have judged me; but when I turned a community event into political theater, I was challenging my fellow Americans to choose whom they would serve: Are you on the side of God or the side of the devil? Are you on the side of the adulterer or the side of the chaste? Are you with the sinners or the saints? Strangely, I had never thought of asking the sinner his opinions myself, in a serious conversation where I listened instead of combating. In fact, I had never had a serious conversation with the damned because, in my safe world where everyone thought like I did, I never met them.

I attended a church where everyone was not only a Republican but a Republican who submitted to my parents' biennial cajoling to man the GOP phone bank in support of pro-family candidates. We did not attend public school or listen to rock music or wear faded jeans or watch movies made after 1955 or dance to anything except for our worshipful interpretations of Rebecca St. James or make friends with those who did any of the above. A public-schooled family came to our church for a while, but we stared at them pityingly and felt we had nothing to say.

For four days every February during the state legislative session, my fellow homeschoolers and I trooped to the state capitol in our uniforms of khaki pants and denim dresses to learn about the inner workings of government. We gathered outside the governor's office to pray that our leaders would turn to God again, we heard talks about how a biblical worldview leads to a belief in limited government, and we learned that polarization creates debate, and debate is good. We learned that the essence of cultural engagement is confrontation—badgering people into a corner to defend their beliefs, even and especially if it makes them uncomfortable.

I proposed serious bills for our mock legislature—that we should take educational power from the state government and return it to local schools, for instance—while others proposed that Snickers bars should become our organization's official candy or that older siblings were forbidden to commit PDAs. I wanted to debate my serious bills so we could converse about the purpose and role of government, but staff members shoved them to the bottom of the stack so they could teach us clever maneuvers to crush our opponents, a goal they could accomplish only by pitting us against one another and stoking our quarrels. They knew we would fight to the death not over abortion, an issue on which we all agreed, but over M&Ms versus Almond Joys. Without controversy no one fought; and if no one fought, then no one learned anything about winning in politics.

At night after our regular classes, we learned how to browbeat heathens into faith. Our adult leader, Bill, taught a foolproof apologetics tactic that did not actually require you to know anything—perfect for fifteen-year-olds whose main contact with atheists was confined to ten-minute disputes. Bill was not above donning a wizard costume to represent the forces of worldly wisdom, but underneath his jokes lay a deadly seriousness. In a social setting you got the sense that he'd prefer to sidestep chitchat for the thrill of asking a Marxist how he would feel about being wrong if he died.

Bill's foolproof strategy centered on the Four Killer Questions: *What do you mean by that? How do you know what you are saying is true? What difference does it make in your life?* And the sobering kicker: *What if you are wrong and you die?*

This approach didn't require you to refute, or even know, the tenets of Marxism or socialism or secular humanism because you strictly limited your conversation to asking these four simple questions again and again. If the Marxist responded with the same questions, you shot back, "What kind of evidence would you accept as proof?" Since we'd learned that his objections weren't serious or even intellectually honest, that they were grounded in nothing but a stubborn blindness to truth, the Marxist could give just one honest answer: "None."

To demonstrate the implementation of the Four Killer Questions, Bill showed a video of himself using a man-on-the-street interview style at a street fair. He would approach someone who had taken sides against God—perhaps a girl in a spaghetti-strap top in a Planned Parenthood tent or someone manning a New Age booth studded with crystals—and unleash the Four Killer Questions. These conversations usually ended with the person throwing Bill out of the tent. This was fine with Bill.

"I am not a 'nice' Christian," Bill announced. He said that by "nice" he meant "stupid," a definition from the thirteen hundreds.

The Four Killer Questions brought the godless to Christ—later. Those Four Killer Questions would gnaw away at the girl from Planned Parenthood or the guy with the dreads, eroding their faith in their worldview until someone else dropped along with the gospel message, which Bill could give in precisely two minutes using his watch as a prop.

The implementation of these Four Killer Questions was tricky, however, something like an elephant trying to put a thread through the eye of a needle. The staff informed its young charges that this week they had invited as our guest speakers several non-Christians against whom we could wield the Four Killer Questions. Many of us had never seen a Democrat before and were eager to convert one to a Christian Republican using our newfound arsenal of deadly queries.

The first victim was a woman who gave our group a pedestrian talk about what a legislator does all day. When she paused, a slender youth in a navy blazer, impatient to turn the talk to more vital matters, raised his hand and went straight for the kill: "What do you think about abortion?"

The woman replied that it was important to respect different viewpoints on such a controversial matter, but she did indeed support a "woman's right to choose."

A girl in a long khaki skirt bobbed up: "What do you mean by that?"

Bemused, the woman explained.

"How do you know you're right?"

The woman said something about how a woman's right over her own body took precedence over a fetus that could not survive without her.

"What do you mean by *fetus*?"

The answer did not matter; it only served to clear the way for the next question. A boy whose ambition was to rule the world by the age of thirty lobbed the next grenade: "What difference does it make in your life?"

The woman's voice got testy as she launched a volley about back-alley abortions. The class director got up, stood politely behind her, lifted his hand, and said, "One more question!"

"What if you're wrong and you die and you've killed thousands of babies?"

We gave the speaker a standing ovation because the staff had trained us well in the ways of politeness. The woman stalked out, forever leery of speaking to Christian "leadership schools" again, and I stayed safe from the taint of her sin and free from having to listen to her story.

I SPENT A YEAR AT COMMUNITY COLLEGE believing that standing up for Jesus meant making myself the most obnoxious student in class. I struck a deal with God, promising that since He gave me a job at the local newspaper and wanted me to stay in New Mexico, I would speak out for Him. In my classes I argued that Social Darwinism led to the Holocaust. I said that Christianity was the only possible foundation for democracy. I noted that the Native Americans did savage things, and that was why the pioneers dubbed them savages. I agonized over whether I should speak up or shut up and struggled to hear God's whisper every time my teacher said something liberal.

And then I burned out. The belligerence drained me. The confrontation made my classmates aloof. I ran out of arguments and fled to a more like-minded college to escape the exhaustion of constantly defending my faith.

During one of my summers home from college, I worked at a library with heathens who wore ugly clothes, had large hair and glasses, and liked books—a passion I shared. We painted our supervisor to resemble a statue for an educational library program, ate chocolate-covered locusts to get kids interested in books, dressed one another up as Dora the Explorer to pique the interest of the young ones in learning, and got together for picnics in the park to play Ultimate Frisbee. After we became friends, my parents invited them to our home, and we built a campfire, roasted s'mores, and sat around talking until late at night. On one of those lazy summer evenings, I realized I'd lost the compulsion to argue people into worldview compliance. Although our Christian friends exhorted us to do our duty by creating conflict where there was none, I never unleashed the Four Killer Questions.

I didn't chide my friends for swearing or sinning, and I abandoned the need to be always, forever, noting how other people were wrong. They knew we were Christians by the books on our bookshelf, the picture on our wall that showed a father praying over his child's bed surrounded by angels, and the plaque that said, "As for me and my house, we will serve the LORD."[3] For once, I wanted just to care about people as people—not as enemy combatants, potential converts, or notches in my holy belt of truth.

At the end of that summer, my sister left for college and one of the boys wrote her a message that said our family had helped him believe again that people could be good. It was so much more rewarding than conquering the San Juan County Fair Annual Goat Costume Contest for Christ.

4

The Shining City's
Superman

*I*t was clear on day one of our homeschool speech class that our instructor, the head of the San Juan County Republican Party, was training us up to be GOP operatives. And it was clear in the final days of the class that I was up to the challenge.

"And for our final exercise, we will have a minidebate competition. And for the resolution... Drumroll, please!

'Resolved: that Ronald Reagan was the greatest president of the twentieth century!' "

He held aloft the prize, a calendar featuring Ronald Reagan pictures alongside quotes from the Great Communicator. I promptly died and went to a heaven where there was no more dying and no more tears, no progressive income taxes, and no American Civil Liberties Union. No Democratic National Committee or William Jefferson Clinton. Where the Gipper sat at the right hand of Jesus, who sat at the right hand of God. When I returned to earth, I knew only one thing mattered: I had to have that calendar.

Some children revere saints. In the conservative circles of my childhood, we had heroes—not suffering martyrs who sacrificed for their faith but conquerors who crushed the enemies of God with truth and justice. These conquerors had to be Christians, preferably of humble roots and always of stainless character, who overcame their enemies to accomplish deeds that changed the world. We read glowing heroic accounts that omitted Thomas Jefferson's deism, Louisa May Alcott's transcendentalism, and Christopher Columbus's avarice.

Choosing a hero was imperative, and mine was Ronald Reagan. I devoured every book that canonized him and gulped down his 752-page autobiography. I collected his movies: *The Hasty Heart*, in which an angry Scotsman bests him for the broken heart of an angelic nurse; *Bedtime for Bonzo*, in which he parents a monkey while accidentally winning the affection of a charming farm girl. But the crown was *This Is the Army*, a patriotic epic in which Reagan plays an entertainer who joins the army and discovers his assignment is to put on a musical show to boost morale. The harrowing twist is that he refuses to marry his girlfriend because he doesn't want to leave her a widow if he gets killed in action. On the slender peg of that quandary, the director hung scores of army-themed musical numbers. I was so enthralled that I wrote a review of the film on Amazon.com, encouraging the skeptical buyer in tones redolent of an auctioneer: "If you like dear old sappy corn-ball musicals that teach old-fashioned, out-dated lessons like patriotism and love of country, *This Is the Army* is the show for you." It featured, I added, "the greatest president since Teddy Roosevelt as a supporting actor."

The show combined Ronald Reagan with a second-tier hero: the patriotic songwriter Irving Berlin. Berlin penned "God Bless America" and wrote a musical called *Miss Liberty*, along with a song that went, "Hats off to America, the home of the free and the brave." He even made a cameo appearance in *This Is the Army*—as a tiny man walking out on the stage and singing flatly, "Oh! How I hate to get up in the morning. Oh! How I'd love to remain in bed."

I read a biography of Irving Berlin but grew uncomfortable when he joked about having sex on his honeymoon. The coarse jesting meant that he didn't fit the "stainless character" criteria of a hero, and despite penning "God Bless America," he was Jewish and not an actual Christian; my ideal was a hero I could one day meet in heaven. Ronald Reagan's biographies, on the other hand, did not mention sex. They mentioned he had a divorce, of course, but skipped the part where Nancy Reagan was three months pregnant before they got married—a detail Peggy Noonan did not overlook in her memoir of the Reagan years. Shocked, I dismissed it as salacious gossip and chalked it up to Reagan not being a Christian at the time. I had read no record of a Damascus Road conversion experience, but I assumed it must be in there somewhere. I glossed over the parts where Noonan talked about how opaque and distant Reagan was, just as I somehow overlooked the aching loneliness in the words of his children, who wrote about how he always seemed so distant. Though Noonan and others tried to show Ronald Reagan as a three-dimensional human with flaws, to me he looked like a medieval icon of a saint—flat, suspended between heaven and earth.

In my speech class we were debating the greatness of Ronald Reagan, not because anyone disagreed he was great but because we had to know our enemies' arguments if we were to defeat them. Whenever our speech teacher asked, "Why do we learn speech?" my hand shot up: "To learn to give a defense for the hope that's within us!" I was quoting the apostle Peter, who was speaking of the gospel.[1] But to me the hope of the gospel meant more than the truth that Jesus Christ, fully God and fully man, had come to earth, died on a cross to free us from sin, and then rose on the third day. It also meant the hope of being free from the shackles of government as we worked to redeem the world for Christ through political means. I read Jesus's words in Luke 4:18: "The Spirit of the Lord is on me, because he has anointed me to preach good news to the poor. He has sent me to proclaim freedom for the prisoners and recovery of sight for the blind, to release the oppressed."[2] When I heard "freedom," I thought "deregulation of onerous government rules"; when I heard "blind," I thought "blind to the virtue of limited government"; when I heard "oppressed," I thought of children who were not allowed to pray in school and successful rich people whose money was seized by the government. I would whisper, "It is for freedom that Christ set us free," and would think, *Freedom to display the Ten Commandments in a public place!*

And Ronald Reagan was, as the preeminent conservative and the *sotto voce* speaker of an innocuous civic faith,
the earthly bringer of this good news. His story proved the
truth that one person had the power to mold our nation into
the kingdom of God if he had the fortitude to stand against
the axis of evil, cut taxes, and build up nuclear arms. I read
a biography of Billy Graham and felt that he and Ronald
Reagan, the evangelist and the politician, shared the same
heroic beginnings and the same heroic ends. They were
both down-home boys with humble starts, one from North
Carolina, one from Middle America's Illinois. Ronald Reagan restored America to its economic and moral and political glory, while Billy Graham brought the nation to its
knees. I could do the same for my own generation if I was
only open to God working through me, if I could give great
speeches full of great thoughts. An ordinary girl like me,
devoted to God and country, could, if the Almighty willed,
change the world.

And so this semester-long speech class was a practice
drill for my ultimate mission. I skipped the speeches about
my favorite foods and what I did for summer break and cut
straight to the political rhetoric that would prepare me for
my destiny. I gave speeches on the power of words to change
the world (using Ronald Reagan as my prime example), on

why George W. Bush should be the Republican nominee for president (comparing him to Ronald Reagan), and on why public-school students should rise up against tyrannical administrators who forbade prayer in public schools. Before my speech teacher announced our final debate, I had given a speech on why Ronald Reagan was the greatest president since Teddy Roosevelt. I burnished this speech ceaselessly, digging through the thesaurus to festoon my nouns with adjectives afresh, locking the bathroom door to practice before a mirror, and mincing for facial expressions that conveyed the passion flowing from my heart. I was the greatest communicator of the Great Communicator's greatness.

That calendar should be mine.

A few days before the debate took place, I had the chance to defend my arguments before opponents who didn't just pretend to disagree. We had my grandparents over for dinner—a set of urbane atheists who had birthed a couple of disappointingly religious nuts in my mother and her older sister, a Russian Orthodox nun. My grandmother once wore a button that said "I believe Anita Hill," the woman who accused conservative Supreme Court nominee Clarence Thomas of sexual harassment. When my sisters and I mentioned we were working hard on our speeches, our parents seized the opportunity to squeeze in some rhetorical practice. "Why don't you give your grandparents one of your speeches?" my dad asked.

I mentally ran through my repertoire, realizing that I was now forced, by the limitations of my earlier rhetorical exercises, to take a stand for truth and seize the moment to witness for God and Republican values. The time to share my hope with the unconverted had come. *When the Word of God goes out, it does not come back void,* I reminded myself[3]—and besides, their criticism would help hone my arguments for our Reagan debate. So I printed out the latest draft of my speech on why Ronald Reagan was the greatest president since Teddy Roosevelt.

As my grandparents settled onto the couch, I took my place behind the large stereo speaker we used as a podium, my belly quaking a little. My deaf grandmother always boomed her outrage at a volume I could not match, at which point she would bellow, "Speak from your diaphragm!"— an order we never quite executed to her satisfaction.

I cleared my throat and opened my eyes wide as my parents had instructed when I'd practiced my speeches before. Hand gestures were still beyond my preadolescent oratorical skills, so I anchored my fists to my sides and lobbed my cause: "Ronald Reagan stood before the vast, huge, thick Berlin wall and said, 'Mr. Gorbachev, tear down this wall!'

And Mr. Gorbachev did tear down that wall." I described how Ronald Reagan had inspired Americans to be "happy, joyous, and proud to be Americans again." He was great because he had destroyed the "evil, inhuman wrong Communist empire." And most important, he believed in God.

I ended with his quote about "a shining city upon a hill," which I'd committed to memory: "I've spoken of the shining city all my political life.... In my mind it was a tall, proud city built on rocks stronger than oceans, windswept, God-blessed, and teeming with people of all kinds living in harmony and peace."[4]

I sat down, trembling with the thrill of suffering the persecution sure to come, but my grandparents merely applauded. My mild-mannered grandfather was too polite to match his seventy-five years of honed intellect against that of a twelve-year-old. My deaf grandmother had not heard a word.

Afterward I attacked my debate research. My sister Dawn and I were fortunate enough to be assigned the side that argued Ronald Reagan was the greatest president of his century. For the next week I lined up the Ronald Reagan facts I'd collected to build our case. He was greatest because he was a good Christian man of character. He was greatest because who in the twentieth century could possibly be greater? Not Franklin Delano Roosevelt, since he'd expanded the reach of government during the New Deal.

When the day came, my sister and I took our places behind our table, and I sized up our two opponents. Daniel was a massive youth with an imposing physical presence, but when our dad said, "I just think girls have more natural verbal skills than some men," he was speaking of Daniel. Mark, by contrast, was a gentle soul whose goal was to become a veterinarian. He had a habit of walking my mom out to her car and carefully closing her car door behind her. She always said, "Well, thank you, Mark," and as we drove off, my dad would say, "He's such a nice kid, but it's a little too much."

No doubt, my sister and I were sharper and feistier. This would be an easy victory.

The boys, as born conservatives themselves, knew it was impossible to argue that Ronald Reagan was bad, so they argued instead that he was not quite as good as Theodore Roosevelt. I debated brilliantly, argued passionately, painted a deft picture of Theodore Roosevelt as a progressive who instituted unconstitutional national parks and set big government in motion. I dipped into my brain and drew up fistfuls of Gipper trivia, skewering each of my opponents with the force of truth.

After we gave our rebuttals, I waited impatiently for our

teacher to announce the winner, anguishing over the thought that the calendar might adorn Mark's wall or, even worse, kick around the room of someone who wouldn't give it a place of honor. "And the prize goes to the Affirmative team, which has proved that Ronald Reagan was the greatest president of the twentieth century!"

I took the calendar, cupping Ronald Reagan's face in my loving hands. My sister and I would enshrine his image on the wall of the bedroom we shared, but he was really all mine.

A few months later someone at church trying to make conversation hit on a topic they knew I loved and casually mentioned some news I found devastating. A liberal media outlet had taken a poll on who was the greatest president of the century. Of the choices offered, Ronald Reagan came in last. I ranted and raved to my family in the car on the way home, seething at the idiocy of my fellow Americans. The next day I collared a mother at speech class to inform her of this travesty. She politely extricated herself by saying consolingly, "Well, at least *we* know the truth."

But her response wounded me as much as the poll. For the next few days, I was brimming with tears, my heart breaking for the foolish Americans who had ranked Ronald Reagan last, not because they were malicious but because how can they believe in the one of whom they have not heard? And how can they hear without someone preaching to them? And why would anyone preach if they thought it was enough simply to know the truth themselves?

In the diary I intended for my future biographers, I answered the mother who said, "At least we know the truth." "It's not enough to know the truth!" I wrote. "Truth is such a precious thing. Jesus is truth, and truth has power to set us free from sin and bondage! Truth is sacred because it's God's and because He is the One who gave it to us and then opened our eyes to see its wonderful worth. Truth is like a treasured book that you've read over and over again, and who doesn't want to share a book with a friend? It hurts when the people you love reject the truth, exchanging it for a lie."

Somewhere in there, I got my gospels crossed.

THE NIGHT AFTER THE 2008 presidential election, I stood on the concrete floor of a warehouselike music hall in Manhattan called Terminal 5. Like the rest of the twenty-something New Yorkers there, I had stood in a long line the day before—in my case, winding around the block and moving slowly toward a dilapidated Brooklyn school—to cast my vote. I was celebrating the end of this long election at a concert. I was ready for an end to politics and ready for the Decemberists to take me back to days of pirate ships, fairy queens, star-crossed lovers, and revenge.

But when lead singer Colin Meloy bounded on stage, he began with a call to Obamamania, rejoicing, "It's a new dawn, a new day!" A chipper guy next to me said the more we cheered for Obama, the better the show would be. They dedicated to President Bush a song extolling former CIA operative Valerie Plame. They danced a cardboard cutout of Obama across the stage and propped him next to a microphone. Later, during a song about a grizzled reprobate being swallowed by a whale, the band sent Obama crowd surfing through the audience.

Meloy spun a yarn about Sarah Palin giving a press conference on her way home to Alaska and kept up the narrative about Bristol Palin and her "unborn fetus" beginning a guitar duel.

"Snap together for progress! Snap together for change!"

The crowd snapped wildly.

"Yes, we can!"

The crowd yelled, "Yes, we did!"

They unfurled an American flag, and for the first time,

I found myself in the Obamamania frenzy that fascinated the media and terrified the Republicans. I'd heard stories of people fainting at Obama's rallies, and I'd seen the John McCain campaign ads flashing shots of crowds at the National Mall shouting, "O-ba-ma!" next to images of Paris Hilton and Britney Spears. I had missed those rallies, yet here I was, after it was over, bearing witness that Obama's name alone could make everyone lose themselves in the chanting.

The Decemberists left the stage, and the applause for the encore began. The cheers built and then the rumble began—"Yes, we can!"—and crescendoed: "Yes, we CAN! YES, WE CAN!"

I had hopes that Obama might be the statesman of our generation, but as the "Yes, we can! Yes, we can!" reverberated to the balcony, one thought gripped me.

I can't.

I had always heard that the Pharisees missed Jesus because they were searching not for a suffering servant but for a warrior king who would come with armies to overthrow their political enemies. How absurd, I always thought, never seeing that I, too, had searched my whole life for an earthly messiah who would overthrow my own political enemies, the one God would use to lead His chosen people in His chosen nation back to Him.

I was done chasing supermen. I had stopped believing in the perfect leader who could say "Let there be justice" and by the force of his word change the whole earth into heaven. Instead I determined to grab hold of the truth I'd always known—that the Leader had already come, had chosen instead to say, "My kingdom is not of this world,"[5] and had been despised and rejected because His message was bigger than the first-century political pundits had predicted. When Jesus said to go the extra mile and turn the other cheek, He called us to subvert tyranny with love and redeem injustice with suffering. He didn't say that tyranny and injustice would cease immediately, but He promised that the time would come when the meek, the poor, and the merciful would inherit the earth.

The Decemberists came back on the stage and played one final number, "Sons and Daughters," a song about people beginning a new life where bombs and dirigibles had no place. It reminded me of Ronald Reagan's shining city, "built on rocks stronger than oceans...teeming with people of all kinds living in harmony and peace." It was, of course, an image he borrowed from Jesus, a vision that originated in the same sermon where He exhorted the weak, the poor, and the powerless to be the light of the world, the "city on a hill" that can't be hidden.[6]

As I pushed my way through the crowd and got in line to pick up my coat, I passed a woman next to the bar raising her beer cup high and singing, "Here all the bombs fade away. Here all the bombs fade away."

One day they will, I thought, *but not today.*

While God Is Marching On

I flipped on the Christian radio station on a Tuesday morning expecting Jaci Velasquez songs and our morning-show hosts giving away Papa John's pizza coupons to winners of trivia games. Instead I heard the serious voice of the host saying a plane had crashed into the World Trade Center tower in New York City. We listened, and when we realized this was no accident, my mom called us all into her bedroom, where we sat on the bed and started to pray.

That evening as we drove to our church for more prayer, I looked out the windows at the faded buildings in my little town and saw more American flags than I'd ever seen before—flying half-mast from gas stations as long lines of cars snaked to the pumps, and from houses and feed stores and hardware stores and the local bank. We pulled into the parking lot of our tiny church, a simple storefront in a strip mall, and we sat down in our usual row of chairs just behind the pastor's family. As our pastor rose to pray, I realized that this could be the moment I'd been waiting for. A crisis like this could finally shatter America's hubris and make her realize we needed God in our public life once more. As my father began to pray, I closed my eyes and remembered the cloud of debris and the smoking towers.

And I hoped. Maybe this tragedy would divert America from her destructive course.

The next day, Leonard Pitts Jr., a liberal columnist, wrote a column that I clipped out of the paper and filed away with other 9/11 mementos. His words burned with a holy anger that I had always thought liberals incapable of: "Did you want us to respect your cause? You just damned your cause. Did you want to make us fear? You just steeled our resolve.

Did you want to tear us apart? You just brought us together."[1] He spoke of America's strength, and I found it strange to see my own patriotism flowing from a liberal's pen.

The newspaper folded over an insert of a paper American flag, and I saw the paper flags taped up everywhere from grocery stores to dentists' offices. The grocery stores sold stickers of American flags with "9/11: Never Forget" printed below. Suddenly, it seemed people everywhere were on their knees. Radio stations pleaded for pastors to come and record prayer for our country and calls to repentance.

The world had shifted in a way I'd only read about in the oldest of the Bible's sacred books. Although ancient Israel backslid, worshiped false gods, sacrificed its children, and neglected the tabernacle where God resided, God never abandoned His beloved. Judgment came, the Israelites in their misery repented, and God always welcomed them back with a heart that forgave again and again. I believed America, the new Israel, was stuck in the same relentless cycle: we backslid, sacrificed to the false gods of Hollywood and big government, murdered our children, and forsook the sacrifice of obedience; but surely repentance and redemption and revival would come before it was too late.

When I prayed for revival, I took literally the biblical injunction to go into your closet to pray.[2] Crouched there among the shoes and the Sunday dresses, I whispered 2 Chronicles 7:14: "If My people who are called by My name will humble themselves, and pray and seek My face, and turn from their wicked ways, then I will hear from heaven, and will forgive their sin and heal their land." On behalf of my countrymen, I confessed America's sins.

We were arrogant. We fancied we could get along without God in the public square. My family once watched a video of David Barton, who would later teach biased history to Glenn Beck viewers, presenting graphs of terrible statistics that showed unwed pregnancies, sexually transmitted diseases, premarital sex, divorce, and cohabitation suddenly skyrocketing in 1963—the very year the Supreme Court kicked prayer out of public schools—while test scores plummeted and violent crime spiraled out of control.[3]

We were depraved. Every week I turned to the page in the conservative newspaper *Human Events* that summarized, in a jeremiad of righteous indignation, all the movies I wasn't seeing and tallied the number of obscenities and profanities in each one. Marilyn Manson's music embedded mayhem into children's brains—yes, even children who were "only listening to the melody"—and drove them into killing frenzies.

We were murderers of the unborn, but that, too, was

part of the cycle. I'd watched a video in which a man spoke of how redemption always follows the slaughter of infants: Israel was rescued after God slew the Egyptians' firstborn, and Jesus came when Herod ordered all the boy babies killed. What glorious act of redemption, the speaker asked, could follow our own nation's slaughter of infants?

I ached with fear for my country. We could choose morality, or we could choose to laugh at depravity. "See, I set before you today life and prosperity, death and destruction," God admonished the Israelites. "I have set before you life and death, blessings and curses. Now choose life, so that you and your children may live."[4]

I knew that revival always began with judgment. Some hellish word or hellish happening—a picture of depravity—was the only thing that could shake God's people from their complacency and jolt their sin-dead hearts into resurrection. I pictured revival beginning with a twenty-first-century Jonathan Edwards in a small church in a tiny town waking up one day and being moved by God to preach an unusual message. He would approach his pulpit that Sunday, look out at the soft sinners sitting in the pews, and then launch into a modern version of "Sinners in the Hands of an Angry God"—a tale of woe, of damnation, of sinners being dangled over the mouth of hell by an outraged deity. That same hand would clutch the hearts of the people who sat rapt in the pews.

First the Christians would fall on their knees, crying out to God in repentance for their apathy. The unsaved would follow, prostrate and in tears. This revival would spread—no one knew why the time was suddenly right, why the moment was suddenly ripe—across the entire nation. Whole classrooms of public-school students would erupt into prayer, and administrators or judges would be powerless to stop it. The movement would sweep up not just a few students but all of them, carried on a wave of fervor that came unbidden and could not be turned back. People would flock to the steps of the Supreme Court and clamor for the overturn of *Roe v. Wade.* Supreme Court judges would suddenly change their hearts about prayer in schools and abortion law. And it all would have begun with a single person—the small-town pastor who woke up one day with the urge to preach a sermon on hell.

As I watched in the days after September 11, I dared to hope that this was it—the calamity that struck us with the fear of hell.

A few weeks after the attacks, hundreds of citizens flooded our civic center for a community call to repentance and prayer. We watched a video montage of images that showed our cultural decadence: riots, men with studded lips and women with garish makeup, two men holding hands, abortion clinics, glass panes with bullet holes. Then images of 9/11 flashed on the walls, not just the images of destruction but the pictures of heroism—firefighters with blackened faces carrying the wounded to safety, the strong shielding the weak from the gray wave of smoke and glass. I rose to my feet with the crowd as the music swelled: *"And I'm proud to be an American, where at least I know I'm free."* Americans were born with a steely strength that, despite all our indulgences in between crises, emerges whenever our national honor needs defending. I was now part of a generation that had died for freedom, and we would find in ourselves that American strength and virtue that our grandparents had shown.

A few weeks later, on Veteran's Day, we poured into the auditorium again to celebrate our troops. Religious leaders stood side by side with civic leaders to lead us in trumpeting patriotism. I stood with the community choir and sang, *"Mine eyes have seen the glory of the coming of the Lord: He is trampling out the vintage where the grapes of wrath are stored."* It was no longer a song for the past but a song for today, as

I saw the stirrings of the glory of revival. *"As He died to make men holy, let us die to make men free, while God is marching on."*

But repentant fervor faded before revival came. Less than a year after 9/11, a local church in my town organized a celebration of America, baseball, and God to evangelize the high-school baseball players who swarmed our town every year to play in the Connie Mack World Series. The church paid a hefty speaker's honorarium to bring in Dave Dravecky, an inspirational Christian speaker and former baseball player who had lost his pitching arm to cancer. He would draw the baseball players while Daniel Rodriguez, the NYPD cop who had charmed the country with his operatic voice just after 9/11, would draw the patriots. But when my family slid into our row, we found that the crowd had not come. A handful of Connie Mack players rattled in half-filled rows, a contrast to the overflowing auditorium less than a year before. As another musician droned on the piano, I found I was not actually indefatigable when it came to patriotic events. In fact, I was bored.

The unthinkable happened, not on September 11, 2001, but on that day in 2002 when I realized American life had lapsed back into apathy. The rallies ended. The radio shows went back to their regularly scheduled programming. The pastors' coalition stopped holding big community prayer meetings, and the paper flags drooped in all the windows. Even I woke up and did my schoolwork and wrote my speeches and went days without remembering after I'd promised I would never forget.

Revival came—and went. And if this didn't birth resurrection, what would?

MY FRIENDS AND I SPENT Fourth of July 2009 in a languor of strapless summer dresses in Prospect Park, New York. We hashed out our complicated relationships for the twenty-seventh time while we stuffed ourselves with hummus and carrots and tortilla chips heaped high with guacamole. As the afternoon waned, we moved the party to a Park Slope apartment and ate cheesecake out of a box before we climbed out a window onto a fire escape and then up to the roof to watch the fireworks. The sun set pink and blue, and the darkness deepened. We saw the Brooklyn Borough Hall clock tower red in the distance and the Empire State Building across the Hudson, lit up red, white, and blue. Those colors were as patriotic as the evening got.

The next Sunday I went to church and found myself sitting through a history lesson packed with statistics I'd heard countless times before: the Founders' writings overwhelmingly quoted the Bible more than other philosophers; when the Israelites voted on leaders to rule over them, it was the origin of the representative form of government; a pastor named John Witherspoon mentored dozens of influential founders and drew his views on government from the very Deuteronomy passage we were reading that day. All true. And all facts I'd been taught to buttress the idea that America was somehow more Christian and somehow more special than other nations—so favored by God that He would always take us back no matter our infidelities.

I thought back to how I'd felt on a Fourth of July six years earlier—the year the war in Iraq began. I wore a gray T-shirt adorned with an electric guitar and a swash of stars and stripes with the words "America Rocks." (The T-shirt had inspired me to write a deadly earnest newspaper column asking if "America Rocks" was too shallow a sentiment and concluding…America does rock!) My family and I encamped with our church on the lawn of the community college for an all-day Fourth of July celebration. We brought out our ancient hand-crank ice-cream maker and took turns cranking the mixer by hand as the melted ice dribbled out a hole in the side. The ice cream came out soft, and we ate big bowls of it quickly with homemade brownies crumbled on top. We hacked a watermelon into chunks and sucked the juice into our mouths as we bit into it, jutting our chins so the juice would drip on the grass. Waiting for the fireworks, I watched the New Mexico sun set purple and gold over the sand as the piñon scrubs turned to black silhouettes on the hill. When dusk came, we pulled out a radio and adjusted the antenna to the college radio station. The lights exploded across the sky, and the beat of the songs seemed timed to the bursts. Tears came to my eyes as the music rose to a crescendo—"From sea to shining sea!"—and the fireworks reached their finale. And I prayed, as I always did, for my country's repentance and redemption.

But in recent years as I've looked back at the breadth of history—the Mesopotamians, the Greeks, the Romans, the feudal kings, the French revolutionaries—I've seen that America's entire existence thus far has taken up just five hundred years of history, which means that some other nation or king was claiming to be God favored before America declared it was God's new light to the world. Before American democracy became the form of government Christians favored, medieval Christians believed God favored the right of a king to rule over his people, protecting them in return for their allegiance and service. The Puritan founder of Massachusetts, John Winthrop, didn't believe we were all equals but that "God Almighty" had made "some...rich, some poor, some high and eminent in power and dignity, others mean and in subjection."[5] He and his fellow leaders thought a truly godly commonwealth should drive out Quakers, Catholics, Baptists, dissenters, questioners. Christians in the antebellum South argued that God endorsed slavery because Paul instructed slaves to submit to their masters. America's empire builders claimed that God gave them the right to pillage Indian villages because God ordained that America expand. Christians today say the Bible endorses capitalism; Christians two hundred years ago said it endorsed the divine right of kings. Both missed the point, which is that the Bible is neither an eighteenth- nor a twenty-first-century policy textbook. It endorses neither the fiefdom nor the global superpower. America is not a "uniquely Christian" nation, and it never was.

My thoughts came back to the sermon when my pastor said in closing, "I hope that makes you proud to be an American. I want you to be thankful today. I want to ask in closing that you rejoice. Rejoice in your country."

He ended the sermon saying, "God bless America." Then

we rose to our feet to sing "My Country, 'Tis of Thee." This was the kind of song we would have sung on that Fourth of July six years ago at my old church back home in New Mexico. The people around me began to sing:

> My country, 'tis of thee,
> Sweet land of liberty,
> Of thee I sing;
> Land where my fathers died,
> Land of the pilgrims' pride,
> From every mountainside let freedom ring!

But as they did, I stood there silently—just staring at the words on my bulletin, angry because I'd come to church to worship God, not America. I thought of how in the past few years I've seen America live out what Reinhold Niebuhr called the "irony of history"—when strength becomes weakness because strength prompts vanity.[6] We went to war against a nation that tortured its political enemies, turning to torture ourselves under the pretext of securing our nation's safety. We liberated a people only to find that they saw us as invaders. In the name of protecting the American Dream by letting capitalists do what is right in their own eyes, we triggered a financial crisis that would make a generation, living in their parents' homes with their college diplomas and empty résumés, feel the American Dream had eluded them. In the pursuit of self-preservation, we abandoned the values that are worth preserving.

But when my church sang on, "Long may our land be bright," I found myself opening my mouth and singing too: "with freedom's holy light." I sang to see if the words could still move me. They didn't; they felt heavy with all the wrongs of the past years. But I kept on singing because I still believe in the ideals of freedom and equality, although our nation so imperfectly executes them. As flawed as our country's founders were, no one has stated the ideal—life, liberty, and the pursuit of happiness—more eloquently.

I now think that loving America is like loving my family. We have a shared identity and a common experience, a history that ties us together and past grievances that divide us. But I don't love my family because it's exceptional, because it can dominate everyone else or has the fastest technology and the richest members or is somehow more blessed by God than others are. I love my family, my country, because it's mine—because this is the community where God saw fit to plunk me and I have an obligation to its rancorous, disputatious, obnoxious, and suffering members. It's easy to love the world and hard to love our neighbor.

In a show of neighborly love, in a gesture toward how things should be, I could sing.

Deliver Us from Evil

My poetry teacher had black eyebrows that looked like a man's and hair as black and thick as horse hair. She wore it parted down the center and loose on her shoulders over flowing dresses in earth tones. Her serenity matched her mien. I could imagine how she might go out in the morning and raise her hands to the sun and then go back into her stucco house on a mountain and burn a stick of incense while she wrote about nature.

We arranged our chairs in a circle because it felt less like a classroom and more like we were peers, although our teacher was a prize-winning poet while the rest of us were students at a community college. I deduced quickly that poetry classes are made up of socialists or maybe Democrats if they lean toward conventional or, at the very least, peaceniks who object with equal fervor to claims of absolute truth that cramp sexuality and to humans raping the earth.

It was 2003 and the topic of war came up in every class. In my speech class we opined about the pros and cons of the war in Iraq. On campus we held a formal debate where one side argued for the war and one against it. I had just learned terms like *preemptive strike,* and once when I drove to school, a few antiwar protesters dotted the side of the highway. I tried to picture my eighteen-year-old friends—computer programmers, debaters, history buffs, nerds—as soldiers and utterly failed, although my grandfather who fought in World War II was as slender and mild mannered as they.

One day my poetry teacher passed around a sheaf of published poems about World War I—the first modern war, according to what I'd gleaned from my history classes, and one that returned a generation of men shattered by the horrors they'd witnessed.

"Alisa, will you read this one aloud?"

I read Wilfred Owen's description of a gassing victim who gargled blood when his fellow soldiers threw him into a wagon. His eyes writhed in his face, "His hanging face, like a devil's sick of sin." If you could see his agony, the writer said, "My friend, you would not tell with such high zest / To children ardent for some desperate glory, / The old Lie: Dulce et decorum est / Pro patria mori."[1]

Dulce et decorum est pro patria mori.

"It means," said our teacher, " 'It is sweet and fitting to die for one's country.' "

James, the socialist who spent most of the class flirting with the only student who counted as a published author since one of her poems had appeared in a local literary journal, smirked. "They still tell those lies."

I FILLED MY CHILDHOOD with sounds and images of war, so romantic and sad. My parents forbade the negative content of most modern movies and boycotted Disney for its portrayal of rebellious, scantily clad heroines, so I grew up as if I lived before the age of color television, watching Laurel and Hardy join the army and listening to big-band music crooned by stars like Bing Crosby, Frank Sinatra, and the Andrews Sisters.

The songs were jaunty, with brass bands swaggering and trumpets ripping through jazz runs, a bass thumping a rhythm you could swing to. The Andrews Sisters, who sang in one of the army comedies I watched, all looked the same, wore identical uniforms with neckties, and somehow danced in sync while wearing high heels and the same broad grin. They snapped in time and sang a song where a lover warns his girl not to sit under the apple tree with anyone else until he comes marching home. In another, a "boogie-woogie bugle boy" goes to the army and plays his boogie-woogie bugle to wake up the troops, ejecting them from their bunks with grins on their faces, ready to fight.

I would lie in bed and listen to the music throb while I fell asleep. Some of it choked with wistfulness, but it was never unhopeful or despairing. You might be gone, it consoled, but I'll still find you in the morning sun and all the old familiar places.[2] The day might be dark, but the lights will go on again all over the world.[3] Free hearts would sing, the world would be infused with love and laughter and peace while bluebirds wheeled free over the white cliffs of Dover.[4] *Tomorrow, when the world is free.*

The music and lyrics answered a longing in me for heroism and sacrifice—that unity around a noble cause everyone believed worth dying for. My generation was so soft and my grandparents' generation so strong and steely. The men were demigods in uniform who died tidy deaths with small smudges of blood on their foreheads and kitty-sized scratches on their lantern jaws. The women carried on nobly at the home front, wearing trim suits because fabric was scarce, drawing lines up the backs of their legs so it looked like they were wearing pantyhose when there was none to be had, and winning the war as riveters with hair perfectly curled and lipstick so deep and red. They were heroes too.

I loved the photos of my grandmother and grandfather from that time. My grandfather leaned on the railing of a gazebo, sharp in black and white, and looking, as they said back then, like a "dreamboat." My grandmother's snapping brown eyes flirted with the camera. I would have cast them as romantic leads in a film about a sweetheart waiting for her man to come home so they could sit under the apple tree when the world's lights turned on again.

But one day I popped in my grandmother's big-band cassette tape and heard a song that pricked me with uneasiness. A gunner fell and the sky pilot set aside his Bible and took up the gunner's gun, singing, "Praise the Lord and pass the ammunition, and we'll all stay free."

I hit Fast Forward, scrambling the buoyant trumpets and brassy tune. It was all right to portray the long-suffering nobility of soldiers writing letters to their sweethearts and thinking of home or even the soldiers fretting about their girls sitting under apple trees with other men. But with this song I could see the gunner lying in pieces and the sky pilot using the phrase we all toss so casually—"Well, praise the Lord"—before he used the ammunition to rip a hole in a human being.

This discomfort pricked me again when I watched *Sergeant York,* one of the patriotic movies Hollywood made during World War II when the Office of War Information was in every studio reading all the scripts and encouraging studios to ask of each one, "Will this help win the war?" In the movie, Alvin York, a real-life World War I hero played by Gary Cooper, is a hard-drinking, sharpshooting redneck until the Lord, quite literally, strikes him with lightning and the jolt shatters his hardened heart. He becomes a church-going man who reads "Thou shalt not kill" and interprets it to mean "Thou shalt not kill even when your country asks it of you." He persists in this error until the army sends their deadeye on temporary leave to reconsider using his God-given ability to serve his nation. York trudges up a mountaintop with his hound and his Bible while the voices duel in his head: "God…country…God…country." Then the pages of his Bible flip open to Jesus's words: "Render therefore unto Caesar the things which are Caesar's."[5] With illumination breaking over his face, he repeats the verse again and again, looking off into the valley. The words have made it clear that he should kill. When he goes into combat, York is unflappable, gunning down a row of German soldiers, one after another, with the line, "Just like shootin' turkeys."

Just like shootin' turkeys—except, of course, it wasn't. The scene always made me prickle with discomfort and wonder why his earlier interpretation of "Thou shalt not kill" made more sense to me than his later interpretation of "Render unto Caesar the things which are Caesar's." I'd always found the phrase cryptic, since it seemed to imply that there are political matters God cares nothing about. "Thou shalt not kill," by contrast, is bald and blunt. I'd always learned to interpret cryptic scriptures in light of those that are clear. I wondered if York had given way in a grave matter of conscience—and even if he was right, did he have to narrate so callously? "Just like shootin' turkeys."

These unanswered thoughts still rankled when I went to our local library, traveled down the stairs to the dank nonfiction section, and requested that the librarian—a rail-thin man who wore his steely hair in a twist tied around with red yarn—help me find books about civil disobedience. I was writing a speech for my homeschool speech tournament, urging public-school students to rise up in acts of civil disobedience and pray in school, but I needed to establish the moral and ethical case for it. He led me to the great disobeyers: Tolstoy, Gandhi, Thoreau, and Martin Luther King Jr., whose moral vision especially gripped me. When I opened a children's book on the civil-rights movement, I saw a photo of three teenage activists crushed against a building beneath the blast of a fire hose, one boy sheltering the girl and another with the shirt and skin being flayed off his back. This picture of nonviolent resistance to injustice struck me as being powerfully Christian, a testimony of how the weak things of the world—love, compassion, forgiveness in the face of brutality—can splinter hate.

I began to wonder, as these writers and Alvin York had before me, how any kind of violence was right, even the romantic wars I loved. I started to think about the twisted glee of victory and how it only comes after we've killed enough people to say we've won. I read Jesus's instruction to turn the other cheek, and it seemed so impossible to interpret in any other way than how Alvin York interpreted it: "Thou shalt not kill even when your country asks it of you."

I asked my pastor about it, and he told me Jesus's injunction against violence didn't apply when we were protecting someone else; in other words, turn the other cheek only if you're the one being slapped. Still not satisfied, I asked my grandfather one day when I went over to his house to heat up dinner. I needed to draw on his wisdom as someone who had actually lived through wars and as someone who, although he was a liberal, I trusted more than anyone else to have thought things through and have a good reason for what he believed.

"If killing is wrong, why isn't it always wrong?" I asked.

"So you're thinking of becoming a pacifist?" He smiled. Strange idea for a kid with a "Bush 2000" sticker on her debate-evidence box.

"It just doesn't make any sense to me that you can kill for a good reason if killing is wrong."

"The problem is that pacifism is noble, but it would just never work," my grandfather said. "People are always wanting power and to exploit other people, and if you refuse to stop them, it just ends in more bloodshed instead of avoiding it. You can't just sit out the fight." He was matter-of-fact and measured. "If you don't fight to defend yourself and your country, then someone else will—or no one will and then more innocent people die."

For the first time in my previously black-and-white existence, I found myself taking up uneasy residence in a world where there were shades of gray. I had to wrestle with two noble ideals in conflict—the call to live in peace and the call to defend the innocent—and wonder if it was impossible to realize both. Jesus taught peace and love and turning the other cheek, but we seemed unable to achieve the "peace on earth" the angels had said His birth brought—not even by voting correctly and electing reasonable leaders with circumspect beliefs. Sin and blood washed over the world and darkened a vision I saw as deeply Christian—that we return violence with peace and show the world a better way.

With reluctance I decided it made the most sense to calculate the human cost of war and the human cost of staying out. If refusing to fight led to even more death and destruction than fighting itself, we should fight. But that tallying of bleeding bodies left me chilled.

NOW HERE I WAS IN 2003 with my country going to war, reading poems about the wounds war causes and the "old lie" that perpetuates it: *Dulce et decorum est pro patria mori.*

I cautiously supported the war because I thought it was about defending our country and protecting innocent citizens from the threat of even greater bloodshed. When someone strikes your cheek, you turn the other cheek. When someone strikes the innocent, you punish the one who does wrong. Saddam Hussein hadn't struck us yet, but he was winding up for mass destruction—or so we were told.

As I read the poem, all my misgivings about the morality of war returned. To steel myself, I looked up the State Department's "Human Rights Report: Iraq" to remind myself what we were fighting for and what evil would be allowed to flourish if we didn't fight. On class day I took my place in the circle of chairs and waited for my turn to read my poem aloud for the class critique.

James launched into his short story—not a poem because that would be too conventional in a poetry class—about two people who met at a bar and felt a mystic connection. They stumbled home and ripped their clothes off, mashing their mouths and bodies together in an ecstasy of soul mating. The kicker: they were both men, and one character was just as surprised as the audience to learn he was actually gay.

It was a strange prologue to mine. When he finished I pulled out the sheet of paper on which I had neatly typed my poem in Times New Roman because it was the best font.

My chest felt tight behind my JCPenney "America" T-shirt as I read.

Human Rights Report: Iraq

The government has a long record of executing
    perceived opponents:
Political dissidents,
Economic saboteurs,
Car smugglers.

The government has a long history of lining men up
    against prison walls and
employing high-powered rifles to drill holes in their
    hearts,
and lungs,
and heads and bellies.

But not before the government inflicts discomfort.

Because the government also has a lengthy history of
branding faces
and snapping legs and arms in two,
and beating,

and burning,
and raping girls,
and burning holes in flesh with acid.

The government's justice could be called
poetic.

Two refugees who smuggled fuel are
soaked in it and lit.
A journalist who tells an anti-Ba'ath joke
spends life in prison.
And those too visible, too loud just
disappear.

And the government moves on,
negligent about improving a human-rights record
    which has been
Extremely Poor
for a long, long time.

And the government executes perceived opponents.

I finished the poem and waited, realizing that what
looked like a poem on the page sounded, when read aloud,

like an excerpt from the State Department's human-rights report, which is actually what it was, just chopped up into lines. The other students were silent. Finally one skinny youth, whose poems were an unnavigable maze of metaphor, spoke up. "It gave clear pictures and used strong language," he said. "But I kind of thought it was...cold."

Despite the underwhelming response of my classmates, reading the report helped calm my moral unease. Obviously we were right to defend ourselves against a dictator who was so clearly evil, and in the process we would bring justice to the raped girls, the imprisoned journalists, the tortured political enemies, and the people whose flesh Saddam Hussein had corroded with acid. War was worthwhile if we were defending the innocents from nuclear or biological weapons in the hands of a madman and protecting the last best hope of people yearning for freedom.

For the rest of the semester, I combed the newspapers, waiting for discovery of the weapons of mass destruction we had gone to war expecting to find. I saw the pictures of Iraqis toppling the statue of Saddam Hussein and rejoicing in the streets and felt reassured—they were welcoming us as liberators. But just before the end of the semester, when I polished my poem for my final class portfolio, I saw pictures of naked prisoners in Abu Ghraib, wearing hoods, standing on blocks, kneeling in a shaky pyramid of naked bodies while an American soldier laughed behind them. I felt the same sickness as when I'd read "Human Rights Report: Iraq." *The government inflicts discomfort* on its enemies. Now that government was our own.

Eight years later, the feeling is even more acute as I read of my own government's dissembling and brutality. Weapons of mass destruction did not exist. The threat we imagined was not really there. The military's own documents show that it has killed thousands of civilians[6] and handed more over to the Iraqi police, whose activities sound a lot like the ones I read about in that "Human Rights Report: Iraq."[7] Some wars do not have shades of gray. Continuing them seems wrong—an irrational attempt to justify all the lives and billions we've poured into winning. Our leaders miscalculated and the result was tragedy, but the result would be tragic even if we kill enough people to say that we've won.

I'M NOT ALWAYS SURE how to react to war today. I can vow to work at Dunkin' Donuts before taking a job as a defense contractor. I can threaten to weep should my children decide to become soldiers. I can choose not to tell the lie that it's sweet and fitting to die for one's country and say instead that it's tragic. But all of these are just taking stands, and Jesus requires something more. Jesus didn't say "People who speak out against war will inherit the earth"; He said people who embody, in their character and soul, this strange and alien value of *meekness* will inherit the earth. He didn't say "Blessed are those who refuse to fight" but blessed are those who make peace. He didn't say "Blessed are those who don't kill" but blessed are those who show mercy. He didn't call us simply to oppose positions that are wrong but to embody values that are heavenly.

The best example I can find is from World War I, when the two sides hunkered in trenches with a no man's land—crisscrossed with barbed wire, embedded with land mines, and littered with the bodies of the dead—between them. Wilfred Owen compared no man's land to "the face of the moon, chaotic, crater-ridden, uninhabitable...everything unnatural, broken, blasted."[8] It was the medics who dashed out to no man's land with stretchers, facing enemy artillery to collect the bodies of the wounded; and it was the conscientious objectors who often chose to be medics. They refused to fight but endangered their lives to mend the wounded and bury the dead. The American Friends Service

Committee, a coalition of pacifist Quakers, formed military hospitals, helped refugees, and later rescued those who fled Nazi Germany. It wasn't that they refused to participate in the bloody business of war or that they shrugged off our enemy's evil; they participated, but in a way that affirmed life and showed mercy.

To be a peacemaker is to take up residence in no man's land and become the person who ministers to the bleeding and wounded left behind, who cultivates and inhabits the broken land.

7

Holes

While the girls my age were coveting the latest handbag from Juicy Couture, I was buying a George W. Bush tote bag. While they were cajoling their mothers into purchasing the latest atrocity that would transform them from demure midwestern girls into Britney "Oops!...I Did It Again" Spears, I was wearing a "W. 2004" shirt—in 2000. While they were papering their school notebooks with *NSYNC stickers, I was pasting mine with

George W. Bush stickers, tidily alternating them with American flags. And while they were e-mailing one another about boys and fingernail polish, I was assuming the mantle of e-champion, which required two things of me: an e-mail address to receive daily Bush campaign e-mails and the indefatigable conviction that I must forward them to everyone I knew.

At moments it crossed my mind—mostly when I was juxtaposed with someone wearing a bitty tank top and tiny frayed denim shorts—that cool girls didn't wear T-shirts featuring an artistic rendering of a fetus next to a Mother Teresa quote: "It is a poverty to decide that a child must die so that you may live as you wish." But older Republicans complimented me for being much more modest and polite and informed than their own kids with their tiny tops and pounding bands. I was not in the cool-kids' club since its morass of membership rules was too difficult for a home-schooled kid to decipher. I was in the grownups' Republican club, which picked the future leaders of America and took down public enemies and viewed outsiders with the same conspiratorial air that the cool kids had in all the teen movies I didn't see because I was much too busy getting into a more important clique. I was Alisa Harris, Christian conservative Republican, and as stridently as I insisted that

Christian came first, it was really *Christian conservative* that came first and *Republican* that came next—because being a correctly thinking Christian always meant being a conservative, and not all Republicans were correctly thinking conservative Christians.

When my speech teacher offered to take my sister and me to see George W. Bush in the flesh during the 2000 campaign, I seized the opportunity as quickly as another girl would snatch up a VIP pass to a Backstreet Boys concert. On the day of the big event, I changed out of the clothes I'd worn for the three-hour drive and slipped into a rust-colored button-up shirt and a black skirt that daringly revealed my legs from midcalf down to my shoes, which had rubber heels so thick and heavy they were difficult to navigate around other people's toes. In my midteens I was partial to styling my front bangs in a sausagelike curl and sousing the sausage with hair spray until crispy. In slavish devotion to maintaining my "look," I toted a curling iron wherever I went—including to see the future president of the United States.

After I'd sufficiently curled and doused my hair, we made our way into an arena decorated in an explosion of red and blue and stars and packed with star-struck fans. As I listened to the music twang and looked at the God-fearing, red-blooded Americans seated near me, I wondered if Bush would live up to everything I hoped he would be. When I heard him speak, would I experience that shivery thrill I'd felt before, the one that made me know—just know—this was the one?

As the strains of "The Star-Spangled Banner" floated through the crowd, I sang along with a full heart. Our senator gave a warm introduction, and Bush emerged, shaking hands, waving, cracking his crooked Reaganesque grin. I applauded and screamed with the crowd, "Viva Bush! Viva Bush!" as he made his way to the podium and waved, leaned toward the microphone, and said, "Thank you." When we quieted and sat down, he gave his stump speech, and I felt that shivery thrill—"Yes, this is it"—although I could not remember a single detail when I wrote about the speech in my diary the next night. As Bush exited the arena, I saw he would pass right next to us, so I shoved my hand through the crowd, leaning toward the barricade. But as he glided by, an obese woman in elastic-waist pants barreled past, shoved me aside, and thrust her hand out. I reached out as far as I could in the crowd that pressed around me. My fingertips just brushed the hem of his sleeve.

It was enough.

A FEW YEARS LATER, IN MICHIGAN, when I enrolled at one of the most politically conservative colleges in the nation, I left my "America" T-shirts behind. I dutifully attended the freshman parties, declining a prowling upperclassman's invitation to a frat party, and ate hot dogs and sang worship songs at the InterVarsity Christian Fellowship retreat. Here I was at a school where all my neat categories were mixed up. Would I be one of the teetotaling Calvinist Baptists who married the harshness of Calvinism with the deprivations of evangelicalism? Would I be one of the honors clique whose wardrobe consisted of glasses, socks with sandals, and T-shirts commemorating each year of the honors retreat? Would I be one of the SAI Girls from the music sorority that attended swing dancing each Friday in order to meet and marry fedora-topped boys from the music fraternity? Would I be part of the hip Christian group that saw frat parties as an excellent witnessing opportunity? The answer is all the above, at one time or another. But I spent the first week clumped up in a group of freshman girls. The second week, I realized the only thing we shared was a fear of eating alone in the cafeteria, so I decided to strike out on my own, to become in this new stage of life the only thing I knew how to be and to do the only thing I knew how to do: politics.

I went to the Source, where all the student clubs set up booths in the college's arboretum with bulletin boards showing pictures of students ecstatically participating in their activities. I bypassed the classics honorary and the forensics team and cut straight to the College Republicans booth, where a heavyset student with black curly hair was passing out "George W. Bush 2004" stickers.

"I want to get involved in a campaign," I told Andy. "I've done pretty much everything. Handed out literature, walked in about a thousand parades, done precinct walking, phone banking, waved signs at polling places, gone to GOP conventions..."

"Well, I'd like to see a résumé," he hedged. "And then maybe we can sit down for an interview."

I signed my name to his sheet beneath a list of freshman e-mail addresses. That night I compiled my political résumé with the hope that I'd find my place in the same kind of clique where I'd been so happy before. But when I told Jacob, one of the only people at Hillsdale College I'd known before I came, that I planned to apply for a position with the College Republicans, he made it clear I'd picked the wrong group.

Jacob was partially responsible for my presence at Hillsdale. I had enrolled in a leap of faith, without visiting the college or applying to any other, because it was the only college conservative enough for both me and my parents. Jacob, a former homeschool debater, was the only person I knew who could give us firsthand information. So my mother and I had called Jacob's mother, and she had made him join a conference call in which we quizzed him as to whether Hillsdale would preserve or undermine my superior morality. I did not want to attend a college with a profligate dating environment where my roommates might engage in sexual relations or drink or fail to study responsibly. Jacob detailed Hillsdale's strict moral code in terms that reassured us that my purity of soul would be preserved. When I arrived, however, I found that Jacob had joined a cadre of boozy intellectuals, and his college life seemed to center on writing poetry, drinking scotch, writing poetry about drinking scotch, and quietly stalking freshman girls in the library. Convinced he had become an alcoholic and was possibly dabbling in apostasy since he was absent from the InterVarsity Christian Fellowship meetings, I took to earnestly praying for his salvation and asking my father about the signs of alcoholic dependency.

We both worked at the library—I at the circulation desk

and he at the reference desk. He was cool in the "evangelical ex-homeschooler who quotes the *Aeneid* in Latin while drinking whiskey and smoking a pipe" type of way, which was not very cool in a campus where one of the sororities was nicknamed "Kappa Kappa Visa." I fell even shorter of cool in my chenille sweaters and Jordache khaki jeans. But he did his best to steer me toward hipper choices.

"Don't do College Republicans," he said, leaning against the circulation desk. "Everyone says that College Republicans is the second-largest student group on campus after InterVarsity Christian Fellowship. That's only because everyone signs up freshman year because everyone is a Republican, and then you can't get off the list. But only half a dozen people actually do anything, and they're all weird. You have to be careful who you align yourself with because that's how everyone thinks of you for the next four years."

I pondered this information, unsure whether I should trust someone who was killing his brain cells with whiskey and failing to attend Thursday night worship. But a political activist was all I knew how to be. Back home my family comprised nearly the entire staff of the San Juan County campaign for George W. Bush. They recruited and manned the GOP phone bank and walked precincts with the precision of soldiers. My siblings led the Pledge of Allegiance at

Bush rallies, and my dad had his picture taken with the De-
cider himself. But as I looked back on my ballot stuffing at
GOP primaries and my sign waving and the miles I'd
trudged through suburbia, I wondered if I was picking politics only out of loyalty to my former political self.

Four years after I screamed, "Viva Bush!" at the next
president of the United States, I felt my identity had worn
away against the grit of reality, and now I was featureless.
September 11 had come and gone without bringing revival.
The wars in Afghanistan and Iraq had come and stayed.
The myth of weapons of mass destruction had dissipated
before the sharper image of humiliation and torture at Abu
Ghraib. Despite Bush's declaring "Mission accomplished"
when we took Baghdad and "Let freedom reign" when we
turned sovereignty over to the Iraq people, the nation was in
chaos instead of peace. We were approaching one thousand
dead American soldiers, and when I allowed myself to think
about it, I had no idea what I thought about any of it. All
those old identifiers—*conservative, Republican*—couldn't
sum me up when I was secretly angry at my Republican
president for tricking me into supporting a war and then
changing the reason for invading to a cause I hadn't signed
up to cheer for.

If I asked myself what Ronald Reagan asked voters

when he was first elected, "Are you better off than you were four years ago?" or as the pollsters would say, "Do you feel that the nation is headed in the right direction? Are you optimistic about the future?" the answer was no, not really. I'd been fighting my entire life for change through politics. But I had seen no real change—no mass civil-rights movements for the unborn, no revival sweeping the public schools. I tried to explain my disillusionment to my parents when they wanted to know why my interest in campaigning had waned, and I found myself repeating an idea from Bush's stump speech. Bush had said that when it came to abortion, we had to change not just laws but also hearts. Politics only goes so far, he'd said, and I was beginning to think it didn't go far at all.

But who else could I be if not Alisa Harris, Christian conservative Republican? I missed the camaraderie of the campaign trail, the excitement of the race, the certainty of belief, and most of all, the sense of purpose—the thrill of fighting for something bigger than myself. I was lost without it. I felt blank. Maybe one more presidential campaign could bring that passion back and remind me who I was.

I sat down with Andy in the snack bar, the province of poetic types like Jacob because smoking was permitted, and we regarded each other through the haze.

"Your résumé is good," he said. "Lots of experience. But since you don't have any experience actually running a campaign, I'm going to give you one of the smaller campaigns." He handed me a campaign bio for the Republican candidate for county assessor, then ran through the list of campaign events. I skimmed the biography, realizing that all I really needed to know was that she was Republican. I checked my heart for a surge of the old enthusiasm. Nothing.

On a gray day not long afterward, I roused myself from Saturday-morning dreams and piled into a borrowed school van with the rest of the College Republicans. After the two-hour drive to a larger city, we met Stephanie, whom Jacob had described as the feminist moderate ex–College Republicans leader who had wrested control of the campus's only authentically conservative publication to promote liberal GOP candidates. She passed out enormous T-shirts emblazoned with the name of a candidate I'd never heard of.

The upperclassmen dropped us off at lonely roads, and

we trudged down them, shoving literature into the mail-boxes we passed and then turning around to come back to the waiting vehicle. When it started to drizzle, we took turns dashing out in the rain. Everyone cheered as a freshman un-loaded the last piece of literature and sprinted back to the van, poncho dripping.

When we started the long journey home, I closed my eyes and pretended to sleep with my head against the win-dow, seeking quiet. As everyone else debated the campaign's vagaries with academic precision, I veiled my political angst and wondered how much I had in common with the rest of them, except that we were all flapping red, white, and blue literature for candidates we knew nothing about beyond the *R* next to their names.

A line from one of my political heroes, Peggy Noonan, kept echoing in my mind: "Beware the politically obsessed. They are often bright and interesting, but they have some-thing missing in their natures; there is a hole, an empty place, and they use politics to fill it up. It leaves them some-how misshapen."[1] The observation had always left me un-comfortable, wondering if I were the politically obsessed type with the hole in my nature, but now I knew what she meant. Politics felt hollow, and so did I.

A few weeks later the donors came, and with them came the college's partisan panoply. Over six hundred rich and ancient conservatives poured into campus to be feted, meet the students who had benefited from their largesse, and launch a $400 million capital campaign. The orchestra played a patriotic concert, and the college announced it had created a searchable online database of the writings of William F. Buckley Jr. The college presented an award to a former official from the Reagan administration, unveiled a statue of Winston Churchill, and applauded wildly when Pat Sajak—the face of *Wheel of Fortune* and one of our most dedicated celebrity supporters—read a letter from George W. Bush, saying that Hillsdale College "helped ensure a bright future for all." Then everyone attended a three-day lecture series centered around the theme "Ronald Reagan and the Sesquicentennial of the Republican Party."

Peggy Noonan's line about the "politically obsessed" came back to me when we all filed into the sports arena holding tickets for the keynote speaker, Ann Coulter. I once regularly read Ann Coulter in the conservative tabloid *Human Events*. My parents had given me a gift subscription to the publication, which I had consumed religiously but now tossed aside unread. I didn't care for Coulter's style even when I agreed with her views, but maybe encountering her vigor—her certainty—in person would reignite my passion.

Coulter teetered onto the stage on her long legs and stilettos and launched into a speech ripped from her latest book. She shot zingers that ricocheted and echoed off the walls and around my brain and then disappeared. She left us with no point deeper than "Liberals suck!" As I walked out into the brisk Michigan air, I thought Coulter illustrated the way politics can leave the politics-obsessed misshapen, with no deeper thought than disgust for their enemies. When Dan Quayle spoke the next morning, I couldn't summon the enthusiasm to go to another political speech, so I left his ticket on my dresser and slept through his talk.

A few days after the donors came, Andy sent an e-mail asking if I would volunteer to stand inside the classroom building right after lunch on Tuesday, urging people to change their voter registration and vote in Michigan so the GOP could take a swing state. We set up a card table with registration cards. As the cafeteria doors flew open and students streamed from their lunch to their one o'clock classes, I positioned myself in the busiest hallway and piped my cause.

"Change your registration!" I said as a posse of ham-handed jocks stumped past.

"Vote in Michigan!" I told a group of sorority girls teetering by in high heels.

No one cared. As I stood there, I realized I didn't care either. Why was I trying to sway this stream of people so that I could help elect someone whose shoddy intelligence gathering had duped me into supporting a war I now found immoral? And when it came to the county assessor campaign and the candidate whose T-shirt I'd worn and whose name I'd forgotten, what was the point of working for a candidate I didn't even know? Did it really matter whether the county assessor was a Republican?

I'd tried to summon faith in the redemptive power of politics, but going through the motions made me realize I had lost that faith, perhaps irreparably. The rituals of speeches and signs felt empty to me now. That day I packed up the card table and returned the blank registration forms without bothering to fill one out myself. My mom badgered me, asking where I was going to vote that year—New Mexico or Michigan? The deadline for registering in Michigan floated by. "You should really get your absentee ballot," she urged me. The deadline for requesting an absentee ballot floated by.

Election Day passed quietly. I didn't vote. I didn't think it mattered.

Our hyperpoliticized culture reduces us to solely political beings, defined only by our political characteristics and which special-interest group claims to represent us. Our gayness, blackness, whiteness, femaleness are not parts of a complete identity but our whole identity, elevated from an accident of birth to a political credo. We become misshapen when all the spiritual and intellectual parts of our identity become merely political. We reduce all the complexities of our nature and experience to a political stereotype: the soccer mom, the gay-rights activist, the young white evangelical.

A liberal-arts education is supposed to make you fully human—balanced and whole. Through the mulling, debating, and passion of the classical writers, you gain a fuller understanding of yourself as an intellectual, emotional, historical, and heavenly creature. There's something about it that takes you out of this particular political moment and places you in a bigger world.

And so I put aside the stifling label of Christian conservative Republican and set about molding my lopsided character with literature, history, and theology, learning to love them for their own sake instead of forcing them to serve a political end. I learned Greek. I read Dante, Herodotus, and Gerard Manley Hopkins. I gave earnest theological lectures to the campus's debating society and tried writing short stories. I eventually became the Teetotaling Theologically Ambivalent Christian Feminist Honors Program Enrollee who attended a Baptist church but was not Baptist, who would smoke but not drink, who would admit she enjoyed Nicholson Baker more than John Milton, and who only read the news when forced to do research for the extemporaneous competitors on her forensics team.

There was only one of me on campus.

8

Judge Not

I emerged from the subway in the part of the city where New York University students venture for tattoos and cheap pizza. My small-town self had grown accustomed to midtown Manhattan, where people in suits bustled and tourists with backpacks ambled, but here vendors hawked obscene T-shirts and karaoke blared. Racing the setting autumn sun, I hurried past the hipsters I still couldn't distinguish from criminals until I arrived at the apartment where I would experience my first New York City Bible study.

A group of people, mostly older than I, were wedged into couches and curled up on the floor of the tiny apartment. An enormously pregnant woman did the hostess honors, waddling her way through the tangle of limbs to set out cheese and crackers. After making my introductions I sat next to Ben, a guy who had leaped over a pew the previous Sunday to make my acquaintance.

We launched into the study on the importance of Bible reading, a practice that I, as a proper Christian, already believed in. As an erstwhile Bible-study leader and a model Bible-study participant, I answered the leader's questions with smoothly articulated and perceptive answers, drawing connections between disparate passages, not letting a pause hover too awkwardly after his questions but also giving slower people a chance to answer so as not to monopolize the discussion.

Midway through the discussion a woman breezed in, her curly black hair bouncing around her face and sturdy shoes protruding from beneath her slacks. She was late, she explained breathlessly, because she had just come from a campaign meeting for Hillary Clinton.

I was startled.

As Donna settled into her chair, she made some disparaging remarks about Barack Obama's inability to trounce the Republicans and praised Hillary Clinton's experience, as if her audience would be keen to know which candidate could beat the GOP. She was engaging in a political discussion during a Bible study, not an uncommon occurrence for me except that opposition to abortion and gay marriage apparently didn't fit into her political framework; if they did, she would not be campaigning for Hillary Clinton.

I glanced at the leader, almost expecting him to issue a gentle rebuke or at least indicate that the rest of us were more concerned about deciding between Mike Huckabee and John McCain. But everyone just reached for more gourmet crackers and Brie while Donna said, "What'd I miss?"

We turned back to the topic of Bible reading, and Ben expressed a sentiment I found vaguely heretical: "I actually think I get more out of praying than out of reading my Bible. I just feel closer to God that way." It seemed brazen to say you got more out of one spiritual exercise than another when God ordered us to do both.

A few weeks later Ben advanced once more after church, quickly steering the conversation to the things I liked to do and then suggesting we do whatever I liked to do together sometime. We met a few days later at a coffee shop where suits from Credit Suisse, one block away, folded themselves into coffee-colored booths and blustered into flirtations with skinny girls. I meticulously timed my arrival so I could buy myself a cup of tea before he turned up, so we could avoid the awkwardness of wondering who would pay.

Ben ticked through a litany of questions. How many siblings? Was I raised in a Christian home or a recent convert like he was? Where did I work? What did I do? I mentioned that my job as a journalist at a Christian magazine was to tell the news with a uniquely Christian perspective and, in doing so, betrayed our assumption that "uniquely Christian" equated with "Christian conservative."

"I'm a Democrat," he said.

I took a sip of tea to avoid responding.

"I just always was one," he said. "Everyone in Rhode Island is a Democrat, and I just don't think Republicans care all that much about people." It was the kind of thing someone would say if he spent all his time swallowing whatever CNN fed to him in a spoon, I thought. I believed it debased religion to use proof texts to support political beliefs that Paul and Moses had never conceived of; but still, there were moral issues—abortion and gay marriage—where faith could not help but inform one's political choices. If you were a Christian, you were pro-life, which meant you were Republican. There was no other way. And what about the onerous burden of government regulation and the importance of sound economic policy? Being a Democrat meant thinking shallowly.

I had arranged with my roommate to see a movie in Times Square, so I told Ben I had to say good-bye. We hugged and he said, "We should do this again sometime."

"Yeah," I said, smiling weakly, unsure how to break the hard truth: I would never date a Democrat.

When I talked to the leader of the fellowship group the next Sunday, I dodged the real reasons I couldn't continue by telling him I was looking for something a little bit closer to home. What I really meant was, "It scares me to walk past tattoo parlors." And that I thought it was easiest to be friends with Christians who shared my essential beliefs that lower taxes and less regulation led to a free-for-all of prosperity. If a Christian disagreed, they viewed the whole world in a different way, and then what could we possibly have in common?

JUST A FEW MONTHS EARLIER, right after I graduated and before I moved to New York, I sat between my parents and listened while our pastor and a church elder explained how my own sin required them to stage an intervention.

The pastor and elder, part of a loose affiliation of fundamentalist churches, had grave reservations about women attending college when God ordained marriage and babies instead. College had changed me, they said. I talked more about careers and academics than about being a wife and a mother. They had read my blog and were worried about me filling my mind with *The Office* and Ben Folds. They feared that I would go out on dates and said I was no longer the kind of person they wanted their daughters to emulate. Anger and sadness festered as I picked at the worn blue threads on the couch and contrasted this scene with memories of playing capture the flag with my pastor's kids and of my pastor speaking at my high-school graduation party. But child rearing is simpler when kids are small, before we all grew up and my parents urged us to leave the shelter of their home and go out into the world, while the other families in our church grew more fearful and guarded, keeping their children close.

The winter after this conversation, I went home for Christmas and came across the blog of two brothers, both fundamentalist pastors, who shared my pastor's belief that an unmarried woman should stay in her father's home, not venturing out into the workplace to submit herself to an employer or professor, until she could submit herself to a husband. If the day never came, she would live with her parents and nurse them in their dying days. One headline intrigued me: "Hillsdale Grad Stands on the Word of God." I clicked on the title and found the pastors denouncing a presentation by a faceless feminist from Hillsdale College who, the pastors wrote, thinks that God's Word has "little to no application to our modern, sophisticated, egalitarian, evolved, educated, world." She was "willing to give up Christ as the head of the church," they chided; she rejected "the clearest ethical teaching in the entire new testament," and deserved this warning: if we reject the doctrine of female submission, "there is no ethical teaching of the New Testament which we will not feel free to subvert when we dislike it."

I was the faceless feminist. I had actively celebrated International Women's Day and once led a bra-burning protest to express our rebellion on a campus where most women came for a ring by spring and seemed to think frenzied cooking was the way to get it. We crept into the arboretum at night and cast unmentionables (not our own bras but a small collection we had bought at the annual rummage sale) into a dorm trash can and lit them all on fire. The burning varnish on the inside of the wastebasket sent off toxic fumes, bringing a sad end both to our protest and the can, which we left smoking in the arboretum. I was the founder of an informal association called Hillsdale Christian Feminists, which uproariously shared initials with the campus's Christian behemoth, Hillsdale Christian Fellowship, and was formed in opposition to the Hillsdale Christian Chauvinists, which was formed to mock the campus's saccharine chivalry.

The outline of the feminist presentation matched exactly one that I'd given the previous year and then sent to a friend who wanted to give a presentation denouncing me. The target of their condemnation was unmistakable. They wanted to mess with a college-educated woman in possession of a biting wit and open wounds? Oh no, they didn't.

I huddled close to my parents' wood stove while I banged out a response on my blog. I wanted to be taken seriously as a three-dimensional person—a real human being with a story and with nuanced thoughts, not a faceless caricature they could bat around. I knew fathers in my church who abused their families because they thought their gender gave them license to domineer. One of my friends ran away from her family and broke ties with her father just so she could have a job, go to college, and date a man she loved. I knew another girl who had run away because her stepfather repeatedly raped her. And I had seen all these men somehow drawn to this tiny church that preached men should lead and women submit. I sat through sermons where the pastor said we should train our children—but especially our sons—to be spiritual warriors, as if women's warfare was battling a grimy kitchen instead of the forces of darkness. I sat heavy in my seat while the pastor invited the men and boys, but not the women, to pray for a teenager going on a mission trip. Women probably shouldn't be missionaries, said the pastor's kids.

I wanted those bloggers to know that I had chosen my position carefully, based on a convincing interpretation of Scripture that said verses like "let your women be silent in church" were written to a particular church in a particular moment of time, to advise that church how to avoid being a stumbling block to its culture. Now the opposite—forcing women to be silent in church and denying them certain ministry roles just because of their gender—made our churches a stumbling block to a culture strikingly different from first-century Asia. I was not promoting a system where husband and wife struggle for domination but a system where each submits to the other in Christ, putting their spouse's and children's well-being before their own ambition. I was convinced that if I could persuade any happily married patriarchal man to take an honest look at his own marriage, he would realize it was already working in exactly that way despite all his rhetoric about being lord and master. I wanted the bloggers to know that I was not thoughtless just because I thought differently—that I had lived all their ideas out and seen the pain they caused. So I posted my response on my blog and left the link in a comment at the brothers' blog, letting them know that the faceless feminist was having her say. They fired their shot. I fired mine. We could call it even.

My dad read the post. "Are you sure you want to do this?" he asked. "You don't know these guys. They fight dirty. I really don't think you want to get into a public debate with them. It'll just go on and never stop."

My anger had softened, and I knew he was right, so I disabled comments on my post as a signal that I didn't want to perpetuate any war; I only wished to defend myself after being attacked. When the pastors wrote asking why I'd disabled comments, I dashed off a quick reply saying I didn't want to get into a fight. Truce?

Just after I hit Send, I noticed my embedded work signature at the bottom of the e-mail—that of a Christian news publication read by the kind of people who also read the brothers' blog.

The next day, the blog's front page crowed, "The latest

hire," followed with the news that I—the latest hire at my Christian workplace—was not repenting from my "trendy rebellion against God's Word." They published the personal e-mail I'd sent them along with a carefully edited version of my post, stripped of all Christian content and nuance to make me look like the spawn of Gloria Steinem and Margaret Sanger. Then they provided a link where people could "welcome" me to my new Christian workplace.

As the comment threads on my employer's Web site exploded, I watched and sobbed, racked with the anxiety that this misstep would cost me my job. One reader found it disconcerting that the magazine would hire "someone who seems so opposed to what is clearly Biblical teaching" and said my perfidy was serious enough to make him reconsider subscribing to the publication. A reader who thought the brothers treated me badly still called me a heretic. The nicer posts said I needed prayer and older, wiser Christians "who can speak into her life before she falls deeper into what truly is error." I had agreed with my employers to say nothing until the situation blew over, so I agonized while readers attacked me, left another e-mail from one of the brothers unanswered, and felt further outraged when he explained he was not asking people to attack me but rather wanting his readers to communicate to my employer "their concern that someone who so clearly rejects the authority of Scripture is hired to do editorial work there."

It all ended but left me chastened—determined not to let dogma swallow up my personality and poison my sense of charity. I promised myself I would remember that people are more important than clinging to beliefs I, a fallible being, might have wrong. When I was tempted to say, "You're different, and that makes you wrong," I would remember the people who attacked me, and I would stop.

AND SO I FOUND MYSELF more willing to let Christians hold alien creeds—such as the government should care for the poor—that other Christians didn't hold. And I began to discover that the Bible study I visited didn't house the only Christian Democrats in New York City. They were everywhere.

I read a curious study that said there are quite a few of these strange creatures who don't quite fit in.[1] Young evangelicals have been leaving the Republican Party. They are more conservative than their peers—still very pro-life, still less likely to be Democrats—but they are less conservative and less Republican than older evangelicals. It made me wonder, since there were certain things I didn't love about Republicans, if there was room for paradox in my politics, too.

One morning after the all-female Bible study I'd finally chosen to join, I mentioned these research results to a friend. She was a Pilates instructor who was several years older than I, but we'd both suffered similar wounds at the hands of Christians.

"I can relate to that—not feeling completely at home in the Republican Party," she said as we sipped our coffee.

"There are things about the Republican Party that I just don't agree with, like the war. The war has been such a disaster." I paused to take a bite of the sesame bagel with cream cheese that I ordered every Tuesday, then continued. "And I think that the Religious Right is degrading religion for its own political ends. But then there are things about the Democrats that I just don't agree with either, like abortion."

"But why couldn't a Democrat be pro-life?" she wondered.

What a daring thought. Republicans were anti–big government, pro-life, and pro-marriage. Democrats were against all the things Republicans were for. But was there anything about being a liberal that actually precluded someone from being pro-life? Could this strange political hybrid actually exist?

We bent our heads together over my laptop and searched for the phrase "pro-life Democrats." They had a national organization. They ran for office. They lobbied to change the Democratic platform and—what's more—pro-life Democratic voters elected them. In fact certain districts were so solidly Democrat and solidly pro-life that their constituents wouldn't vote for anyone else.

Intrigued by the unthinkable notion of loving God while believing in a social safety net, I called Donna, the Hillary Clinton campaigner I knew from the previous Bible study. Donna was the greeter at our church service every Sunday. She set out the bagels and stood at a welcome table before and after the service to greet everyone boisterously. When it was time to lift up our prayers and thanksgivings to God, she always had something to say. She jumped on people with bear hugs.

So why was an enthusiastic Christian also a Democrat? "I'm not like a clear-cut Democrat or a clear-cut Republican, but in this world they make you pick a party," she said. She was one of those liberals who view themselves as moderates because everyone they know is even more liberal than they are. When she said, "Fiscally I'm very Republican," she must have meant relative to her fellow blue San Franciscans, because she didn't understand why a country as big as ours couldn't get its act together and provide universal health care. Jesus said to visit the sick and feed the hungry, she observed, so why not put those issues first?

When it came to abortion, she believed abortion is wrong but that the state can't criminalize it. It's a decision a woman has to make on her own without the state enforcing morality. "The whole gay thing?" she added. "Jesus never mentioned homosexuals at all. I just feel that Jesus's heart was more for the impoverished and the sick. I don't feel like He would get so flared up." She thought of herself as a fiscal Republican, a social Democrat, a pro-lifer who didn't believe in banning abortion, and a Christian who didn't think Jesus cared so much whether people were gay.

When I wrote about Donna for an article on young evangelicals, she thanked me: "I still sound relatively Christian!" And to me—someone worn out by Christians who questioned my heaven-bound status every time I disagreed—she was a good one. She welcomed me.

I FOUND MYSELF MORE WILLING to believe that people can hold blends of belief that seem incongruous to someone else. I could be a Christian and a feminist; someone else could be a Christian and a Democrat. But few others seemed to share this perspective. A group of pro-lifers attacked me when I wrote a story that didn't give sufficient space to a pet theory, contradicted by the World Health Organization and the National Cancer Institute, that abortion increases the risk of breast cancer. After I jumped too hastily to criticize a national Christian leader, his PR team continued to attack me after the correction was published. More e-mails, more letters, more long comment threads asking why I couldn't stop being so wrong.

I grew weary. Shell-shocked, I developed a posttraumatic stress disorder that induced acute paranoia and persecutory delusions. I imagined a network of Christian mafia sequestered behind closed doors, commenting on Christian blogs and talking on AOL Instant Messenger, using light pink backgrounds with dark pink letters and with avatars that said "I ♥ JESUS." I was convinced they believed it their Christian duty to hunt down all heterodoxy—all closeted feminists, all secret *Sex and the City* fans, all people with

Democratic friends, all Christian landscapers who cut gay people's lawns.[2] A secret and lethal army skilled in online guerrilla warfare, they would spring into action at the first signal from their leaders to stamp out the faithless among them.

I went into deep undercover and began to lead a double life. I kept my private blog but erased my name and my hometown. I searched out all the places where I'd linked my name with my blog address in a blog comment and sent e-mails asking the bloggers to delete my comments. When someone commented on my blog and used my name, I redacted it. I deleted my siblings' names from my posts. I Googled myself to make sure no one could link Alisa Harris, Christian reporter, with Alisa Harris, feminist liberal.

My mother was worried.

"What would you think about getting some counseling?" she asked on the cell phone as I sat on a rock in Central Park, full of angst. "I just think it might help you work through some things." The next day at church, I cornered a friend who counseled homeless drug addicts and pressed her for a recommendation.

Not long after, I walked in to see the shrink who would exorcise all my neuroses. Her dark highlighted hair fell delicately over her soft white button-up shirt. She wore a tan skirt and sling-back shoes in a neutral color. I primly sank down in the big black leather chair, and she curled up her feet on her own overstuffed armchair.

I started out polite and professional, striving to articulate my neuroses concisely—until I broke down. "I think if my readers knew who I really was, they would hate me, and I'm always scared they'll find out and attack me. I mean, I know it's irrational, but it really is rational, right? Because they attacked me before. And when I make a mistake like this and I let my personal angst spill out, it's not like just a few people see it." I was beginning to melt. "When I make a mistake, everyone sees it, and everyone can attack me, and I just feel like I can't really be myself at all or have any kind of personal opinion, but I just have to conform to this idea of what everyone thinks a good Christian reporter should be."

I turned to the Kleenex box resting solicitously at my right hand for such lachrymose moments, and cried.

We seek in one another the assurance that there is just one correct interpretation of the world, that everything is so simple anybody can see it unless they're malicious or stupid or willfully ignorant; and we punish one another for proving with our differing conclusions that truth is not that easy. We think we must suppress dissension to present the unified front we need to gain power over our enemies. But there are pro-life Democrats, pro-choice Christians, feminists who love their families, and conservatives who care about poor people. Not all of them are right, but neither are they heretics.

Thus—after two years of therapy, after wondering if a tattoo might be a nice quiet way of rebelling against the upright people who seemed to have such impossibly high expectations of my orthodoxy, after forgetting to update the blog that once prompted hotheaded posting and anxious self-Googling, and most of all after learning that it was possible to agree and debate and still stay friends—I try to hold my dogmas loosely. And I never debate without honestly wondering if I'm wrong.

A More Perfect Union

I was pawing through the sales racks at the Gap clothing store, just down the street from the Empire State Building, when my mother called to tell me about the family's elating experience at a McCain-Palin rally. After listening to her praise the speeches, I sputtered out a complaint about Sarah Palin's anti-intellectualism while examining a pair of wool trousers.

"Are you voting for Obama?" she asked me. "You can't vote for Obama. Promise me you won't vote for Obama."

"I promise you I won't vote for Obama."

I lied.

The next week on our biweekly podcast about the week's news, my Web magazine planned to discuss Palin, as everyone did in those days. Before the podcast I called my mom to ask why people adored Palin even after she stumbled in her interviews. My mother said she hadn't seen the interviews, but she liked that Palin was pro-life and didn't sacrifice her femininity.

"Promise me you won't vote for Obama," my mother said.

"I promise you I won't vote for Obama."

When your mother sees straight through you, I'm not sure it counts as a lie.

A few weeks later I talked to my fourteen-year-old sister on the phone. "Dad wants to know who you're voting for," she said. "He keeps asking me if I know. Who are you voting for?"

I huffed that my vote was a private matter. She agreed and said she didn't know why they asked her these things. My mother sent an e-mail saying she would accept my vote as long as I voted my conscience.

That was the trouble—finding the candidate who could encompass my conscience's competing demands. My thoughts kept turning back to an essay by Andrew Sullivan, a heterodox conservative blogger who wrote that Obama alone could take us past the culture wars. Obama alone "offers the possibility of a truce" because of who he is—how he spoke of religion, how he spoke to the world, how he spoke of his own identity. Sullivan's words kept resonating with me as I tried to decide my vote: "When humankind's spiritual yearnings veer between an excess of certainty and an inability to believe anything at all, and when sectarian and racial divides seem as intractable as ever, a man who is a bridge between these worlds may be indispensable."[1]

When our spiritual yearnings "veer between an excess of certainty and an inability to believe anything at all," he was talking about me. The desire to shake off that "excess of certainty" made me unsure of everything. In February I thought I would vote McCain. After Palin's rocky debut I decided not to vote at all. In September I registered as an Independent, just in case, and found that I had no voting issues left. I refused to make abortion my single-issue voting creed. I didn't care about stopping gay marriage, having long ago decided that it wasn't the government's job to preserve what the church considered sacred. I thought tax cuts for the middle class made more sense than tax cuts for the rich, but I felt lost when it came to economics because each side claimed its own ideas would bring economic prosperity, and I had little idea how to sort out opposing claims.

I knew just one thing: I opposed the culture warriors' civil war—the way they fought with no thought of compromise, the resentments they dredged, the mud they slung wildly, the conformity they demanded of their soldiers, and their inability to believe that someone could disagree without being an enemy of the state. Liberal feminists were unable to grasp that pro-lifers might actually care about women. Pro-lifers refused to believe that chastity pledges might not be the most effective form of birth control. Christians obsessed over displays of the Ten Commandments and whether store signs and employees said "Merry Christmas" or "Season's Greetings." Liberals like Bill Maher mocked religious belief, equating it with substandard intelligence and a rural gaucheness.

Obama seemed to transcend this war. He respected even when he disagreed. He didn't mouth savageries to palliate either side, whereas Palin snarled every culture-war standby and McCain—who once took bold stands—now parroted the same clichés.

While I wavered, the world fell apart. Bear Stearns failed.

Lehman Brothers flopped. The stock market crashed, and pundits batted all these new terms: *Moral hazard. Bailout. Too big to fail.* I read articles with ugly words like *recession* and *unemployment.* When I asked myself whom I would want in charge during crisis, who demonstrated those classical virtues—prudence, justice, restraint, and courage—that would ensure he weighed all the options and decided on the best, the choice was clear. People complained he saw too much nuance, mocked him for saying it was beyond his pay grade to answer the question of when life begins, needled him for suggesting he would talk with dictators instead of bombing them—but it all showed prudence and restraint. For eight years we'd had a man of action at the helm; perhaps it was time for a man of thought.

"But what about abortion?" a friend asked as we stood in the lobby of the Empire State Building after recording one of our podcasts. A convert to Catholicism, he was conscious of his faith tradition's emphasis on social justice and care for the poor. "I mean, I'd consider voting for Barack Obama too, but I just get hung up on abortion. If abortion really is wrong, it seems like it's important enough to actually be a single-issue voting factor."

But I liked the way Obama respected those beliefs even when he disagreed. He said, "There is a moral and ethical element to this issue. And so I think anybody who tries to deny the moral difficulties and gravity of the abortion issue, I think, is not paying attention."[2] I was under no delusions that he would overturn *Roe v. Wade,* but neither did Reagan or Bush. And I wanted someone who could take us past our *Roe v. Wade* obsession to talk about some of the other ways we trample human life.

In October I was wandering home from church with a friend. We talked about politics and wrestled with our votes. I was leaning left. He was leaning right. We wound through Union Square, where New York City enshrined Obama with booths that sold Obama art, Obama T-shirts, Obama buttons. Aging African American women walked through and collected Obama portraits to put in their collections.

Then I saw it: a light blue shirt with darker lettering that said, "Blondes for Obama."

"That's my shirt," I said. It spoke to me. It said, "I am a blonde and I am my own special-interest group, like lesbian Latinas or gun-toting Irishmen." It took a stand without taking itself too seriously. After I walked off with my new shirt, my friend said, "Well, I guess you've made up your mind then." And at that moment I realized I had. For the first time in my long and illustrious political career, I was throwing my support to a Democrat—but really I was voting for a leader who reflected my belief that the world is a more complicated place than a culture warrior's sound bite. And I knew that if I chose wrongly, it wouldn't be the end of the world. I'd seen that politicians had their limits in enacting good; they also had their limits in enacting harm.

But Barack Obama's other supporters saw in him not just a chance to end the culture war but a chance to score. On Election Day 2008 I sat at a dimly lit table at Le Poisson Rouge in Greenwich Village. I ate milk and cookies like a fresh-faced youngster while the people around me ordered Palin Pigs in a Blanket from menus featuring three-hundred-dollar bottles of champagne. I watched as a comedian strutted onto the stage in a purple sequined dress and then as busty girls bounced onstage, overflowing from flag bikinis.

"So, Pennsylvania," the comedian cracked when that state's polls closed with a McCain-Palin lead. "Pennsylvanians voted for McCain so they could all have matching comb-overs. They could win a lot more states if Cindy McCain promised Botox in every pot."

For just once in my life, I wasn't the person taking an awkward public stand. For the first time I wasn't the one wearing the GOP T-shirt to the Democrat party or the one clamming up when the comedian yelled, "Who are we here for?" and the crowd roared back, "Obama!" I finally fit in—

and yet I didn't. I voted for Obama because I thought he was above all this political evisceration, yet here were his supporters mucking gleefully like Rush Limbaugh after a Bill Clinton sex scandal.

Leaving the comedy show behind, I went a few stops uptown to the Tank—a gutted, white garage painted with graffiti art, where beer bottles were strewn over tables and the crowd had to squeeze between folding chairs. This was my crowd—filled with young, excited voters who believed in "Hope" and "Change" and "Yes, we can." As the electoral map turned red and blue from east to west, Obama came closer to the 270 electoral votes he needed to become the next president. Virginia: blue. Colorado: blue. New Mexico: blue. Nevada: blue. Obama's count climbed to 220. At eleven o'clock the West Coast polls closed. California, Oregon, Washington, Hawaii: blue. As Obama's electoral count jumped to 296, the room exploded into cheers. People leaped in the air, texted, called, hugged, kissed, cried. Strangers seated near me opened a bottle of champagne and passed it from person to person. The germophobe in me relented to the joy of the moment as I lifted the bottle up to my lips and thought, *Why not? I just witnessed history.*

Half an hour later the revelry grew quiet as Obama

walked on the stage in Chicago. A row of American flags flapped behind him in the cold November air while the crowd cheered and the camera focused on a weeping Jesse Jackson and Oprah Winfrey. At the Tank, friends watched with their arms wrapped around one another's shoulders and a stocky young black man wiped away tears. We cheered when Obama quoted Lincoln and Martin Luther King Jr., and again when he praised "the enduring power of our ideals: democracy, liberty, opportunity, and unyielding hope." This was why I voted—for words of charity that included all Americans, even those who voted against him, in a moment of rejoicing that, as Sullivan said, bridged racial divides.

Afterward a man at the Tank pulled out a melodeon, and people clapped their hands and stomped their feet. Some went home to Fort Greene in Brooklyn where celebrants thronged the streets until after 2:00 a.m., chanting, "Yes, we can." In Williamsburg the hipsters threw off apathy and unironically reveled. When I got off the subway in Flatbush, my mostly African American neighborhood, boys in baggy pants and basketball jerseys cheered on street corners next to squalid corner delis. Their shouts sounded strange to me—almost diffident—as if they weren't used to winning and didn't believe it could really be true.

THE FOLLOWING JANUARY I went to the Schomburg Center in Harlem to watch the inauguration, pressing through the crowd to the auditorium where the audience filled all 340 seats less than an hour after the doors opened. It was more diverse than I expected—mostly black, but there were others: me in my conspicuous blondness, a couple of Indian men, an older white couple. I saw a middle-aged black man dressed from head to toe in camouflage. I sat between a waif-thin older black woman in a lavender turban with a long lavender tunic and a black woman named Henrietta. Henrietta sat on a walker behind the last row of chairs in the bottom half of the auditorium, but when the announcer said Barack Obama's name and the audience stood to their feet, she struggled to stand with the rest of us. She seemed to have something in common with the devout black women I saw hobbling toward the bus stops every Sunday in their pastel hats and pantyhose that wrinkled near their ankles: she prayed. As we waited for the ceremony to start, she told me she and others had prayed for this day and held their breath—afraid to pronounce it, afraid to claim victory but praying all the same. Now they had a new prayer, as Henrietta told me, "that people would get together and do the right thing for every human being—work together as one. No color, just people, loving each other and doing the right thing, helping."

In other words, their prayers included me. I thought of how one set of grandparents forbade my aunt to go to the prom with a black boy. I remembered how my other, southern-raised grandmother cooed at black babies and said when their parents were out of earshot, "We used to call 'em pickaninnies. Can't say that anymore." I remembered carrying a box of clothes down the street on the day I moved into Flatbush and one of my new neighbors yelling, "Stay in your own neighborhood." I remembered how people hooted "Snowflake" at me when I walked to the subway and how I'd always shrugged it off, seeing it as a penance for the actions and attitudes of my relatives.

When Rick Warren gave the invocation during the inauguration, Henrietta murmured "Amen" and "Praise God." When he led us in the Lord's Prayer at the end, I chimed in with Henrietta, though my tears made it hard to get out the familiar words. I thought of the many years that vision of "on earth as it is in heaven" compelled activists to push for a glimpse of heaven's perfect equality and justness on earth. In that long fight for justice, this prayer had been a constant, and reciting it united me with the older black women on either side of me and with the generations who'd gone before.

Afterward I walked outside into the chilly air and noticed a woman smoking a cigarette. I asked what she thought of it all. Her great-grandmother was born in 1873, she told me. She took a drag on her cigarette and said, "My mind stretched back to her and the succeeding generation—the world as I've always known it and the world as it's changed. I pray for the future. I just pray for the future. Let's take freedom out of jargon mode and really practice what we preach."

"Did you think he would win?" I asked.

She laughed and the smoke mixed with her breath in the cold air. "I think some of us just held our breaths, and we said, 'Run, baby, run!' And when he made it, we jumped up and down. We didn't pronounce anything, we just said, 'Run—let's see how far he's gonna get.' And he made it to the finish line."

She stubbed out her cigarette and blinked for a moment in the January glare. "It was the first time I stepped away from cynicism for a minute," she said.

So did I. For a minute I glimpsed what I had yearned to

see: politics transcended, the nation taking one tiny step toward heaven's unity. The same thing happened after 9/11 when I saw store windows decked with flags and auditoriums full of people united in grief and faith. Back then I believed that this would last forever and we would work as one for the common good from that day forward. I'd since learned that we are all selfish, irrational creatures—and then cynicism gnawed away at my belief that we could be anything more. But in that moment on that January day, I felt a little of my faith restored.

These are the moments when we realize that history is bigger than we are. The story is bigger than our personal grievances. If we can hold on to the memory of these noble moments, we can become more consistently the generous, open-hearted citizens we sometimes show ourselves to be. In his own first inauguration, Abraham Lincoln said the "mystic chords of memory," when touched by the "better angels of our nature," will "swell the chorus of the Union."[3] These memories, those better angels, can build on the Union Lincoln preserved and start mediating the civil war that now splits us apart.

In blue America they were mocking McCain's combover and Cindy McCain's pinched face. In red America they were cracking bitter jokes about Obama's Muslim heritage and his birth certificate. But I stepped away from cynicism and shrugged off my "inability to believe in anything at all"[4] because I could believe in this: "No color, just people, loving each other and doing the right thing, helping."

An Ear to Hear

I came from the panting heat into my grandmother's house, covered with grime and trickling sweat from hours of backyard weeding. I poured myself a glass of water and watched from the kitchen as CNN flickered its ticker tape of headlines and my grandmother argued with my parents over the usual topic—politics. Lately the arguments had turned into monologues with us sitting and smiling and failing to engage. It seemed so pointless.

"No one can take away a woman's right to choose," my grandmother said. Then she opened her newspaper and looked at it while a pause lingered.

"I'm glad I had an abortion," she said.

She dropped the comment so casually and the moment passed so quickly I wasn't sure I'd heard right. My mom walked in the kitchen and asked me quietly if I'd heard what she said. "I think so," I said. We walked down the hall, and she told me that Grandma had an abortion after having her last child, my uncle.

"She didn't even want five kids, so when she found out she was pregnant with a sixth..."

What if she'd aborted my uncle like she had the sixth? I tried to picture family gatherings without my funny uncle and the cousin who shared a birthday with my little sister. "Wasn't it illegal back then?" I asked.

"She got a doctor to say that if she didn't get an abortion, she would get depressed, but she was depressed when she came back. People react in different ways when they have an abortion. Some people deal with the guilt by admitting they did something wrong, and other people think it'll make them feel less guilty to say that it wasn't really a baby. Your grandma did that."

I loved my grandmother—how no display of mediocrity could budge her belief that we were the most intelligent, most accomplished grandchildren alive, how she spoiled us and never shushed us when we were loud, and how all my memories of her house were sweet ones, from the moment the rich jingle bells tied to the front door clanged when we opened it until they clanged behind us when we left. But she had a stubborn, unyielding core that made it impossible for her to even hear another opinion. There was no conversing with her—only two sides shouting at each other. It made sense now, I thought, that pain shut her heart.

Years later my mom drove my sisters and me to the airport for our plane back to college. We went to a mall and were sitting in the car in the parking lot afterward, surrounded by Wendy's wrappers, when Mom told us she'd had an abortion too—back in college when she was nineteen.

My mother talked about her past so seldom that it felt strange when she did. My dad spoke of his past so much more easily and often. She used to tell her abortion story to pastors they were recruiting to their cause and to women considering abortion, but she stopped talking about her past when we were old enough to understand. She was afraid the truth of her abortion—for kids who knew that abortion was murder—would be too much for us to handle.

"I want to start telling my story again," she said. She didn't tell it to us then—no details about the father or the circumstances or how she made up her mind or how she felt afterward.

Now I wonder what I would have thought if she had told me that story during my childhood. I don't think I could have looked at her and thought, *Murderer,* any more than I could look at my grandmother and see anything except a hurting, guilty soul. The same act compelled one woman to a conviction that abortions had to be legal and another to believe they had to be banned. The daughter faced down grief and begged God for forgiveness; the mother turned away. The same experience made mother and daughter find each other's position unthinkable.

My parents stopped protesting abortion in my early childhood after they had ousted all the county's abortion providers; I hadn't been to a march since I was small. As a teenager I was more passionate about lowering taxes than about outlawing abortion until I went to a worldview camp in Colorado and was seized with the conviction that this was the most important issue facing our nation today. I could find no way to describe the experience except to say, in the evangelical vernacular, "God gave me a heart for the un-born." I read a spate of books about the abortion issue, drafted opinion columns about it, and rehearsed my argu-ments for the day when someone challenged me.

When I was in high school, I stood behind our stereo speaker turned podium with a sheaf of papers in my hand, the passage I was considering for a dramatic reading at our next speech tournament.[1] I bowed my head to show the au-dience I was entering into an acting role, as was our custom when giving a dramatic interpretation for a speech event, and when I lifted my head, I was in the character of a woman who found herself unable to harm a living thing—not a bug, not a spider, not a dandelion. She hid this compulsion to preserve all tiny life around her until one day she found her-self on an outing with her family and friends, screaming at a hawk that swooped down and caught a baby bunny in its talons. Afterward she struggled to emerge from a fragile dream world in which she lived carefully so as not to break or destroy any being around her.

Her husband decided to cure her of this obsession. While they were out on a walk after the rain, he pointed to a bedraggled gopher and told her, "Kill it." Eager to pass this test and please him, she stomped, and all the memories of the child she'd long ago aborted came back washed in blood like the animal she was pounding to death. "It lifted its eyes to my face and asked for life. I trod it down to the dust, down to join my son. I sent him a playmate. My son will say to him, 'Do you know my mother?' "[2]

I choked when I came to the moment the woman remembered her son and the death she brought him and the roaring guilt. I knew that her fragile almost healing was shattered forever, that some part of her soul had died with her baby. I tried to control my voice as my throat grew thick, but I started crying instead as my parents watched with sympathy on their faces.

I never could make it through without crying, embarrassed but unable to stop. Finally I chose instead a dramatic reading of a poem in which an ogre stalked a village of innocent townspeople, demanding to devour their children. The townspeople sent their children off to the slaughter until one villager stood up and said "No more," and the village blocked its gates and starved the ogre. We, too, could starve the abortion ogre that was devouring our young, I exhorted my audience when I introduced my piece. All it took was one person to stand up for right.

BUT THINGS AREN'T AS CLEAR and simple in real life as they are in poems. When I was a new reporter, fresh off the plane from Michigan to New York City, I was told to cover a women's-rights treaty, the Convention on the Elimination of Discrimination Against Women (CEDAW). My assignment was to report on the treaty's treatment of the unborn, not its treatment of women, although the treaty contained not a single mention of a right to abortion. It only mentioned babies to say that both women and men have a responsibility for bringing them up and that a pregnant woman should not experience discrimination. But abortion? Not a word.

The treaty's text didn't matter, my conservative Christian sources told me. The committee in charge of interpreting the document had mentioned abortion rights, and although this committee had no power to make its interpretation anything more than suggestion, they would launch an assault on nations that still prohibited abortion. Of course, the United States already had liberal abortion laws, so the committee wouldn't press our government to change them. There was little evidence that the UN dictated American jurisprudence;

one time the Supreme Court quoted a brief that argued from UN documents, but that was all.

I had expected a more convincing argument—a treaty that promoted abortion rights so emphatically that its endorsement of evil outweighed its promotion of justice, education, and equality. I looked up Afghanistan's human-rights report, just to see what kind of injustice women face around the world. What I read was worse than I'd imagined—not a set of statistics but stories of how a patriarchal society devalued and degraded and destroyed real women. A boy raped and impregnated his sister, but when the girl told her parents, she was the one they set on fire and killed. A forty-year-old husband tortured his sixteen-year-old wife for a year, breaking her teeth with stones and cutting off her nose and ears. Authorities didn't investigate either crime; in fact, police regularly detained women for the crime of fleeing abusive husbands and fathers. One line evoked an image that haunts me today: "Women occasionally resorted to self-immolation when they felt there was no escape from these situations."[3]

In a country where parents lit their wounded daughters on fire, women lit themselves on fire to escape. I couldn't shake the image of a young girl stepping into flames with a despair so profound that she would rather scorch her own flesh than face her own future. I remembered the moments when I was young and felt a passion to go out and leave my small town and do wonderful things for my country, but then felt myself checked at the thought that God actually required me to stay home and devote my full attention to raising future voters. The work was not ignoble, but I still felt sometimes that life would end as soon as I took it on. All the moments after marriage stretched out into a bleak monotony of diaper cream and dreams deferred—a fate I hoped to flee by never marrying, although I sternly told myself that I must marry if it was God's will. In the smallest way I sensed just a fraction of the despondency these girls felt, and I longed for them to know what I had learned—that they had a purpose in life, that God valued them as independent beings with their own thoughts and wills, that they were not the property of men.

But when I asked conservative organizations about these hurting women and what alternative they proposed, their answers lacked consistency. On the one hand they said the UN had no influence to change laws about female violence; on the other it had supreme power to influence abortion laws. In one breath they said the UN lacked an enforcement mechanism to promote human rights; in the next they blamed the UN for stripping America of its sovereignty.

As I listened to an activist articulate her organization's position on the phone, I realized there was no other way to interpret her answers: the slenderest possibility that the treaty might influence abortion law for evil outweighed any possibility that it might influence gender law for good. She had to choose between the possibility of protecting women's lives and the possibility of protecting unborn babies' lives, and she chose the unborn.

I thanked her, asked her to spell her name and give me her title, hung up the phone, and cried for the girls who lit themselves on fire. I opened my e-mail and banged out a message to my editor, explaining that I would have trouble turning this article in without proposing a Christian alternative to CEDAW: "I don't know why I can't seem to find Christians promoting any international human right besides religious freedom and right-to-unborn life. Am I missing one?"

Later that day I opened his response hopefully. He wrote back that lots of Christians were promoting health rights in combating AIDS or malaria, or working for economic rights for orphans and poor women. For instance, he said, in India there was a cross-stitch business that provided jobs for exploited women.

This was a noble endeavor that countered the stereotype

that Christians only cared about abortion and gay marriage. But it helped a handful of women in a nation of over a billion people where only 2 percent of abused women even bothered to go to the police for help. I closed my e-mail and cried again.

And then I wrote the article, the first of many in which I suppressed my own moral outrage, my own sense of credulity, my own pain at the plight of the born—to focus on our constituency's fears for the unborn. I included the facts: in Saudi Arabia, women may not vote, drive a car, or travel by themselves; in Afghanistan, women set themselves on fire. The whole point of the treaty—the plight of women enduring discrimination, even torture, for their gender—took one paragraph of the article. When I read the facts I wrote, they looked so pallid and lacked the force of the pain I felt when I read about them.

Some pro-lifers are blind to the fact that in the battle to defend the value of unborn life, they sometimes devalue the lives of the already born. Later on I read of the United Nations Population Fund's giving to gang-raped Kosovar refugee women some reproductive-health kits that contained equipment to deliver babies, suture women's torn vaginas, and give blood transfusions. But the kits also contained condoms, birth control, and a piece of equipment that could be used either to perform an early abortion or to help evacuate the uterus of a woman who had miscarried—which was enough for pro-life groups to decry them.

"It seems ethnic cleansing will continue," one activist wrote, "this time masquerading under the name of 'reproductive health.'"[4] The Kosovar women were not oppressed, he scoffed; he knew because they interrupted men and had firm handshakes. I look at these examples, and the facts seem stark and clear and deeply distressing: In a situation where they could help women—raped and bleeding women, pregnant women about to bring new life into a situation filled with pain, women who had miscarried their babies on days filled with suffering—these pro-lifers chose principles over people. They deemed the health and lives of women expendable, acceptable sacrifices in achieving the goal of preventing even one abortion.

I am not suggesting either option is ideal or easy. That, in fact, is my point. These questions are difficult. The answers are not obvious, and so there should be some pausing, some angst, some honest uncertainty as people struggle to decide the best course of action. But I see none of this in the press releases and reports I read. Instead I see both sides telling us that to be uncertain, to dialogue instead of rail, is to betray the cause. Both sides strip the issue down to slogans ("Keep your rosaries off my ovaries"; "Your mom chose life") and symbols (the coat hanger and the tiny corpse).

But I hear the angst sometimes. I met a crisis-pregnancy center volunteer in the bottom-floor Starbucks at the Empire State Building. She was chicly dressed, like a graphic designer would be, in stylish boots and a sweater delicately draped. But as we spoke about her work at the center, I found that she wasn't a volunteer with neat talking points about how abortion is murder and needs to be banned.

"I know that people often make this a black-and-white issue, and it very well could be. But the more you're aware of these circumstances and what people go through, I mean..." She trailed off. "I can be an overthinker." She believed that abortion was wrong. That was clear from the Bible, she said. But she was still pro-choice.

Whose side is this girl on? I wondered. The pro-choice side would shun her for working at a center they all considered extremist. They would claim she manipulated and lied to convince women to continue their pregnancies, even though she agreed that the women had the legal right to make up their own minds. The pro-lifers would say that she wasn't thinking clearly, that she was buying into the lies of the culture, that it didn't matter if she thought abortion was wrong; if she didn't agree it should be banned, then she was condoning murder.

But she was living out an ambiguity that almost everyone, except the people on both extremes, feels. I believe that lying and adultery are wrong, but I don't believe in throwing people in jail for it. I find the Westboro Baptist Church, with its "God hates fags" signs, morally abhorrent, but I wouldn't retract the free speech rights of its members.

The divide on the abortion issue leaves no place for anyone to ask these moral questions. We leave no room for thoughtful discussion because we slap labels on people and toss around accusations of hate mongering at anyone who dares to hint that truth may not be as stark as the activists claim.

None of the labels allow this nuance. If I say I'm pro-life, I'm suggesting the other side is pro-death and denying that they may care deeply about women and babies. If I say I'm pro-choice, I'm saying that whatever you choose is neutral to me; I don't care if you abort your child or not—and that's not true either. "Antiabortion" merely says that you are opposed to the procedure, but you can oppose something without believing the government has to forbid it.

WHEN WE TALKED ABOUT ABORTION, my grandmother couldn't hear what anyone else was saying. It was as if she were physically incapable of interpreting the sounds and sentences to be anything but a jumble of incoherent gibberish. But when she spoke back then, I couldn't hear her either.

The night my mother had her abortion, a boy tried to coax her into skipping class to see the musical *Singin' in the Rain*. "Say there's been a death in the family," he wheedled, not knowing what she'd just done. She told me, "I knew it was a death in the family. I knew that a person had died." She is not as involved in pro-life demonstrations as she once was, but she is still the kind of person abortion rights activists would call an enemy; in fact, the last time she went to a pro-life prayer vigil, someone who disagreed threw a Coke at her.

We've talked about the hard choices we make in helping the born and the unborn. She doesn't see why Christians can't support women's rights when some women overseas are treated worse than animals are in America. We talked about how the reality on the ground is different than the rhetoric. She helped start a crisis-pregnancy center, counseled women in crisis pregnancies, and says that of course some pro-life centers encourage women to use birth control next time—just like Planned Parenthood does—although I've never heard a crisis-pregnancy center say that publicly, not even when facing legislation that would force them to disclose they don't provide contraceptives. Why not say it? It would make the extremists pause and, just maybe, start talking about practical ways that both sides can help women.

Jennifer Miller, a young bioethics leader, organized a conference that brought pro-life and pro-choice academicians, activists, abortion providers, writers, and leaders together to see if they could find common ground on abortion. The conference was tense. At times the dialogue fell apart. At the end an activist called Miller a "naïf" and a "rube" for thinking she could pull it off.[5] But she told me we had to keep trying to speak to one another: "Once you stop trying to engage the other, you break the bonds of humanity."

She told me about the moment when two activists—the rosary pray-er outside the abortion clinic and the abortion provider inside—spoke to each other at a panelists' dinner. "Excuse me," said the abortion provider in response to the rosary pray-er. "I'm not violent. I'm very offended by your comment." The picketer said, "I don't think that I'm the devil. Do I have horns coming out of my head?" They saw each other, Miller said, and they spoke bluntly, honestly—a first step.

It is a first step that people took years ago, in St. Louis, when the director of a reproductive health clinic talked face to face with a pro-life attorney and found that they agreed on more than they thought. When a pregnant ten-year-old came to the clinic for help and decided not to abort her baby, the clinic director called the pro-life director and said the girl needed around-the-clock care. Could she help? The pro-life director raised money to pay a nurse to provide that care. The two groups later united to advocate legislation to help treat pregnant drug addicts.[6]

This story proves that sometimes the ethical choice—uncluttered by rhetoric and agendas, focused instead on how we can help this ten-year-old girl or this pregnant drug addict—is clear. We can have ears to hear.

11

Our Daily Bread

My Brooklyn neighborhood was so rough that all the poor and homeless knew to beg elsewhere. But I came out of the subway late one night and just around the corner, a woman in tattered sweatpants held her belly. "Please, miss. I need something to eat."

"I can buy you something at McDonald's across the street," I offered. She shook her head, held out her hand, and groaned. Conservative axioms ticked through my brain:

some homeless actually want to be homeless and would turn down a permanent home and a job if you offered it; giving cash merely perpetuates a social ill and rewards laziness; if you give money, you're funding booze and drugs, not food and rent; don't give if it's only to assuage your own guilty conscience about being well fed, washed, and white; if a man does not work, he shall not eat.[1]

Embarrassed at my judgment, I said, "I'll only buy you some food."

"Please, miss," she held out her hand. I shook my head and moved past, the words "I was hungry and you gave Me no food"[2] echoing in my head. I turned around and said, "Wait," dug in my purse, and brought up a fistful of change.

In a city where hedge-fund managers hustle past homeless people every day, poverty is always close. And living through a recession brings the plight of the poor and disenfranchised closer. Just a few days before writing this, I was running around midtown Manhattan when I saw an old, grizzled black man in a wheelchair, his legs amputated, begging for something to eat. An hour or so later, I rushed down the subway stairs and hurried past him sitting on the ground at the foot of the stairs in the subway filth, making the same plea. Once, I saw a man with a disfigured face, his features collapsed into a blank puddle of flesh. He carried a sign with an aging newspaper clipping that told his story. Deaf people walk down the aisle of the subway car handing out slips of paper requesting money, then walk back up the length of the car, collecting the papers from everyone who won't give, coins from those who will.

And then there are the people who tell the same story in always-dignified language that sounds stilted and rehearsed: *Sorry to disturb you, ladies and gentlemen, but I lost my job and recently became homeless. I'm very hungry. I just need some help to get back on my feet and would appreciate anything you have to give. Dimes, nickels, pennies, quarters, food—anything and everything is appreciated. Thank you, ladies and gentlemen, and God bless.*

A woman, perhaps in her fifties, though it's hard to tell from her weathered face and thinning rust-colored hair, walks one subway line, declaiming her tale in a tone especially redolent with patient suffering, with piteous details that differ with each telling. One thing never changes: she is always recently homeless and just trying to get back on her feet. Once, when she moved on to the next subway car, a businessman cracked that she'd been "recently homeless" for as long as he'd been riding this train.

Sometimes people come on the subway with bags of sandwiches, announce that they're giving them away to anyone who's hungry, and ask whether anyone who is more fortunate would be willing to donate to the cause. The cynical New Yorker in me comes unbidden and I think, *Clever— a ploy to make people think they're legitimate.* I dismiss their sad stories, faintly irritated that they're trying to manipulate me, but also feel a pang of guilt. What if the story is actually true? Whether it's true or not, what should I do?

I used to think that anyone who was poor had only himself to blame, that America is a magical and glorious place so overflowing with opportunity that anyone who's struggling is simply not working hard enough or looking hard enough or finds it more convenient to live off the hard work of others or would really just rather buy drugs than pay rent. I researched stories about whether shelters have beds for every homeless person in New York City so we could prove that the resources were available but people chose not to use them. I followed people who were trying to coax the homeless into coming with them for food and shelter, and I saw grimy, dim-eyed homeless in Penn Station shake their heads or shuffle away instead of accepting help. I went to Christian ministries that were doing work that I still consider heroic. People emerged from these ministries with their lives transformed, so I assumed that was all it took: change someone's attitude toward work and they can claim the American dream.

When you believe hardship is a person's own fault, it's easy to look right through the suffering. One day when I was walking through Brooklyn, I saw a painting on a piece of plywood tacked up on an old abandoned church. The painting showed an old man with a gray beard wearing his red blanket like a mantle. His left hand rested on his knee, and despite his shabbiness, his posture and expression seemed imperial, like a pauper king or artistic portrayals of Joseph the carpenter. You could have added an infant in a bed of hay next to him and he would have looked at home, blinking into the inky sky at a blur of departing angels.

Intrigued, I went to visit the artist, Gabriel Reese, after finding a mention of his work on a blog. He led me into the big garage that doubles as his studio and showed me his next painting—an elderly Asian man wearing a Superpimp T-shirt and a baseball cap.[3] The old man pushed a shopping cart laden with plastic bags and other treasures—a red folding chair, a bucket, a dingy canvas handbag. Gabriel told me that his real-life model had two carts. He'd push one for a block, then walk back and push the other. I looked at the painting long enough to see that the man's shy smile had an impish glint—something I would have missed if I had seen him on the street, since I'd long ago perfected the New York art of looking through people.

"In New York everything's so much in your face," Gabriel said. He saw homeless people in Toronto where he used to live and even did an art project at Tent City, a community of homeless people. But then he moved to New York City and watched how no one looked at homeless people when they walked up and down the subway. He wants people to look twice, to look past the shabbiness and see the spark of the divine in each figure, so he always adds an unexpected touch of beauty to his portraits. The figure in a portrait titled *Prospero* has a hunted look in his eyes, and his limbs are twisted in some kind of pain that goes deeper than the physical—but he holds a red rose in his hand. Another figure, Adam, looks dignified and professorial with his balding head, glasses, and worn khaki pants. The wings sprouting from his back bring to mind exactly what Gabriel aimed for—"If I Saw You in Heaven," the name of his collection.

Moved as I was by Gabriel's images, I continued to see through the homeless—though not without spasms of guilt—because it was easier than letting my mind linger on their humanity and pain. But something changed when I encountered the recession and unemployment firsthand.

Now when I look at the unemployed and destitute, I see what I might become if my life moves just a few steps in the wrong direction.

I WAS SITTING IN THE PUBLIC LIBRARY on a visit home to New Mexico for my sister's wedding, waiting for my little siblings to pick out books, when my phone buzzed. I pulled it out of my pocket to read the text.

"I'm fired."

For a moment I thought it said, "I'm tired." My fiancé was sick and had slept only a few hours the night before flying back to DC. I read the message again.

"I'm fired."

I flouted library rules and hit Call, whispering between the stacks while David filled me in: his publication had decided to downsize. Right when we had a wedding and honeymoon and new apartment to pay for.

When my mom picked us up at the library, I told her the news. "If you're starving, you can come live with us!" she said with (I thought) a barely concealed note of hope in her voice. "You can live in the little house in the backyard, and we'll make sure Vanessa and Elson leave you alone, and we promise we'll give you your privacy."

"Not how I was picturing our first home," I sighed.

For the next few months, David lined up interviews and sent out résumés and heard, "Just one more week," and, "Check in next Monday." A couple of weeks before I flew home to New Mexico to live with my parents for a few months to stretch my paycheck, we were in my sweltering Brooklyn apartment, too hot to do anything but lie still and let the cool breeze from my air conditioner blow over us while we talked about the future. I turned on my side toward him and said, "What if you don't have a job by the time we get married?"

The thought didn't enter my mind that it could actually happen. We could survive on my salary if we lived in a closet and ate nothing but beans—and fasted every other day. I mentally tallied our student loans and tacked another few hundred on to my grocery bill. I could live on couscous and the occasional chicken breast, but David required actual food.

"I can't even think about it," I said. "I can't."

"It won't happen." He sounded sure.

One month before our wedding, with David still un-employed and his savings dwindling rapidly, I'd had too much time to consider our pending poverty. I was in David's tiny Texan hometown for a bridal shower. David dropped by at the end to be cooed over by his former choir teacher and his aunts and cousins. They all told me I was getting a good one. (I knew it.) Between conversations he pulled out his phone and looked at his bank account. An unexpected automatic payment had gone through. He was now officially penniless.

David drove me home in the family pickup truck, and I looked out the window at the rolling Texas hills and the sky. We had to pay for a security deposit on a new apartment. We had to buy wedding flowers and something to put them in. And we had to pay for the honeymoon trip to Paris that we'd bought plane tickets and lodging for before we knew we would be poor. When he took my hand, I looked out the window and blinked but then couldn't help the tears. "I knew this had to happen eventually." I was reminding myself as much as explaining to him. "I knew you were going to run out of money—I just couldn't think that it would be this month when we have to pay for everything."

He pulled up into his family's driveway and hugged me until I stopped crying.

David landed a job just one week before we got married, but the salary was barely enough to cover our bills. I was looking for a new job, so I sent out a hundred résumés, networked and met with connected people, brushed off my suit and high heels, and waited for someone—anyone—to call me back. We coaxed each other out of discouragement, snuck through the subway turnstiles two at a time to pay one fare, and scrimped by on the few dollars left over between paychecks after paying our bills.

At the end of one of those between-paycheck periods, I hurried down the stairs to the subway and plunged my metro card into the gate only to find that I had to refill it. I calculated how much money I had left in my checking account: $3.52. I could put the five-dollar minimum on the metro card and maybe it would draw from my overdraft fund and I would be okay. But when I swiped my card and entered in the amount, it read, "We cannot process your request." I swiped it again—and again and again. "We cannot process your request. We cannot process your request."

I went to the window and tapped on the glass to attract the MTA employee. "The machine won't read my card."

"Broken," she said in the laconic vernacular of MTA employees.

"Can I use it with you?"

"Cash only."

I opened my wallet and unzipped the change compartment to see just a few pennies. "I don't have any cash." She motioned to me to enter by the emergency exit, and I pushed through it just as my train pulled up to the station.

On my way home after my errand, I tried again, hoping it really was the machine and not my card. The words came up on the screen again: "We cannot process your request." I climbed out of the subway and trudged through the snow to a different entrance. "We cannot process your request." I loitered at the credit-card machine, stepping back to let other people use it and then swiping my card again and again.

What could I do? Wait for David to get out of class and then come across town to bail me out with his card? Should I stand at the gate and say the words I'd ignored so often, rushing past the speaker without making eye contact: "Do you think you could swipe me through?" "Do you have an extra swipe?" "Have an unlimited?" "Can you spare some extra change?"

For the first time I felt the kind of desperation that forced people to do that—when you had somewhere to go and really had not even $2.25 for a subway fare. I started rooting through my bag for dimes, nickels, pennies, quarters, anything. I found an old metro card and put it into the machine. "$1.90," the screen read. I needed just thirty-five cents. I scrounged around in my bag and found a dime and three nickels. I reached into one last pocket and pulled out a dime.

Safe until payday.

I'VE BEGUN TO UNDERSTAND the soul-numbing reality that outside forces—those with the power to hire or not, congressmen deciding to lower taxes or extend unemployment benefits, even the parents who raised me—shape my fate. When people talk about the poor being disadvantaged because of their birth, I think of how my parents helped shape me into the person I was when I picked my college and job—and how my current opportunities now depend on their molding of my past self. This is good when you have parents like mine, but how do you tell the sixteen-year-old girl who lives with her crack-addict mom and has never known her father to just be a different person than who they shaped her to be? She can make her own choices, but the person making those choices has been molded by forces not entirely in her control. And so I can't believe that the poor carry all the blame for their predicament because they didn't work hard enough to snatch the American Dream.

When I walk down Lexington Avenue, I glance past the courtly doormen to the glittering vestibules of people who have made it. In the financial district I see people who have made it in their three-thousand-dollar suits and offices overlooking the Hudson. I hear about the expensive nursery schools where they send their children so that they can get them into expensive elementary schools and then expensive middle schools and expensive high schools and expensive colleges that will become their ticket to anything they want to do, ever.

And I come back to the images of the homeless—the gray-haired man with the red robe, the balding professorial Adam with his wings, the hunted Prospero with his rose—and that artist's reminder that we are more than our occupations, our home, our clothes. We have the spark of the divine.

12

Treasure in Heaven

*I*t all started with me feeling obligated to leave the apartment because I had bothered to get dressed on a Saturday instead of spending the day in pajamas. It ended with ABC News footage of me crying and calling names.

New Yorkers like privacy. We've come to terms with strangers—usually smelly and crass—obtruding into our physical space on the subway and sidewalks and in shops every day. (A man once fell asleep on my shoulder on the

Q train over the East River. A band groupie once bounced her hefty posterior an inch from my coffee-shop table.) Even so, when I go out, I expect some personal bubbles to remain unbroken. I may have to be touched, but I don't want to be talked to, hit on, troubled, or to have my equilibrium in any way disturbed.

So when I purchased my coffee and *rugelach*, climbed up on my stool, and opened my book in a quiet Park Slope coffee shop that Saturday, I expected a peaceful interlude untouched by the world around me.

Park Slope, Brooklyn, is where I wished I lived—where brick brownstones rest between churches on quiet avenues, boxes of free books on sidewalks yield Shakespeare plays and George Herbert poems, and organic clothing in children's boutiques costs more than most bridesmaid dresses. And it's where graying Park Slope mothers reign with delicate, manicured fists. The Park Slope mom feeds mashed organic food to her IVF-conceived infant. She speaks to her child as if he were a professional colleague—in flat and modulated tones.

But my peaceful cocoon was shredded by a mother unfamiliar with these local mores. I'd heard about mothers like this, but I thought they only existed in *The Nanny Diaries* or *The Real Housewives of New York City*. This mother was very much here in the flesh, sitting at a table in a gray suit with her papers spread out, when her daughter and her nanny walked in. The woman learned that her employee—a short black woman in the kind of tight, bright yellow shirt you find for $5.99 in the part of Brooklyn where I actually lived—had forgotten to ship a FedEx package. She erupted. As she got louder, the coffee-shop customers swiveled and watched.

"Did you take the dry cleaning? Did you do the laundry? Did you get the dinner? Did you clean the upstairs?" I watched in a sidelong glance as she pounded her nanny's sense of worth to a pulp. I could almost see the bruises blooming. "You're a moron. I pay you too much. You know what else? You eat too much of my food. You're fat!" Her volume rose. She slammed her hand on the table. She grabbed the nanny's arm. The nanny cried, pleaded for the two weeks of pay that was late in coming—and said she couldn't get home without it.

I exchanged shocked looks with the woman next to me. I closed my book and fidgeted with my phone. I looked out the window and tried not to listen. But I felt a familiar tug— the same impulse I'd had at seeing people sit on the subway and cry. Each time I had felt drawn to break my New York bubble and offer sympathy, but I told myself that people don't like anyone to notice them crying. So I would just look away until it was too late to say anything.

This time, I forced myself to turn around on my stool and watch.

"I'm not interested!" the woman snapped at the nanny. Then she pointed at me: "She's interested!" She grabbed her daughter and moved toward the door.

I am by nature a nonconfrontational person. The type who does my roommate's dishes to avoid reminding her to clean up after herself. But this time something snapped. I slid down from my stool as anger—an impulse I'm usually able to check—volleyed forth.

"You're a BITCH!" I shrilled.

All through the coffee shop, people gaped openly as the woman turned at the door and roared, "Why did you call me that?"

"You can't talk to other people like that," I blathered. "You should talk to her like she's a human being. You're abusing her, and I don't care if she's your employee!"

Overcome by my stand, I started to bawl—one impulse I can never seem to suppress—grabbed my bag, and bolted. As I fled, I glimpsed a mix of naked sympathy and embarrassment on the face of a woman sitting next to the door. Maybe I fled because it really is true that we don't like others to notice we're crying. Maybe I fled because I'd run out of words to express my indignation. Maybe I fled because I was terrified.

Then my good New Yorker moment took a twisted turn.

As I stumbled out of the coffee shop, four women clutching clipboards hopped out of a car parked curbside. The *Great footage!* glints in their eyes belied their words of reassurance. "Don't be upset!" they consoled me. They were only reporters from ABC News, manipulating people's sensibilities in the name of "social experimentation," journalistic enterprise, and, of course, mistreated nannies. The whole scene was fake, complete with paid actresses and hidden cameras in the coffee shop.

When they asked to interview me, I wiped my nose and eyes and shook my head, bewildered. Before I could form an answer, one woman firmly gripped my arm (to keep me from wandering into traffic in my distracted state) and led me across the street to a nest of cameras and microphones.

The interview was raw, and shaken though I was, I realized I was still spilling blather. Then the interviewer asked, "Why did you speak up for this woman?"

I gave the only answer I could—not the politically correct or the cleaned-for-television script about recognizing universal human rights. "God made everyone," I said, "and we can't treat human beings like that." In that stricken state I could only go back to the way I was raised: God created every human with equal worth, and that's why we take the stands we do.

"Some people might call what you did heroic," the interviewer intoned. That's when my sense of irony kicked in, and I hoped the producers would put my God comment right next to the footage of me shouting an unsavory epithet.

The interviewer mispronounced my name and wrapped up the interview. Then I half printed, half signed a release form with a description of me—blonde, black sundress, and black flats—and took a business card with the producer's contact info. I walked home and reflected—deflated—that the first time I had the courage to stand up in a crowded room and launch a solitary strike against injustice, the injustice had been staged. And the first time I got on television, it would have to be footage of me spouting rude declarations and erupting into tears.[1]

And yet my whole life had led to that moment. When my parents took me to pro-life rallies and quoted, "Deliver those who are drawn toward death, and hold back those stumbling to the slaughter,"[2] they were preparing me for theatrical clashes of justice and injustice. They opened my eyes to right and wrong, justice and injustice. They taught me that God always hears the cries of the trampled and that He will hold the rest of us to account. Did we weep for the weak?

> If you say, "But we knew nothing about this,"
>   does not he who weighs the heart perceive it?
> Does not he who guards your life know it?
>   Will he not repay each person according to what
>   he has done?[3]

When the moment of injustice came, so came the wrath and then the tears. But now I knew that the next time I saw injustice and the victim was real, I would act boldly. I would speak up for the voiceless.

A COUPLE OF YEARS LATER in April 2010, I slipped through a gate in City Hall Park and merged with a crowd of union workers marching on Wall Street. I was carrying a reporter's notebook instead of a sign. The video screen over our heads showed a preacher in a clerical collar raising his hands as a piano beat a cadence in the background. He yelled, "Are you tired of the banks? Hallelujah!" A loudspeaker blared the Chi-Lites singing, "For God's sake, why don't you give more power to the people?" An older man with a silver beard and sunglasses and a suit carried a sign that said "Trust me. I'm a banker." A cardboard pig—smoking a cigar and wearing a top hat—clutched a bulging money bag labeled "My retirement funds."

A few days earlier I'd watched on television as senators questioned Goldman Sachs investment bankers about their role in creating and selling the financial instruments that helped bring down the US economy. The bankers allegedly sold the financial instruments to investors with one hand and with the other betted against the very instruments they sold—a clear conflict of interest to anyone with a conscience. But apparently theirs had shriveled away. "Did you do something unethical?" the senators pressed. "Wasn't this wrong?" And the men replied over and over again that it was just business.

In more private moments they were less guarded. Fabrice Tourre, one of the investment bankers called to testify before the Senate, sent his girlfriend e-mails that revealed he knew exactly what he was doing[4]—selling a worthless deal doomed to failure. In a sickening turn of phrase, Tourre bragged that he'd sold his worthless securities to "widows and orphans." But in front of the world, he remained coy about his lies.

As I sat on my futon and watched the C-SPAN coverage, my outrage burgeoned. I didn't even care if they admitted it was illegal; I just wanted to see some glimmer of conscience. I wanted one of them to say in front of the United States Senate and the United States citizens who suffered for their misdeeds, "Yes, I was wrong. Yes, my greed brought down the US economy. Yes, I sold bad deals to widows and orphans, and I'm deeply sorry that people are suffering for it." Instead one banker said, "Wrong to me has some qualitative comment about doing something inappropriate. That doesn't mean we didn't make mistakes."[5] But the definition of *wrong* goes beyond "inappropriate" or "illegal." Greed is also wrong, along with manipulation, lying, and taking advantage of unsuspecting customers to sell them what Tourre called "monstrosities" in his more honest moments. The bankers measured rightness and wrongness in dollars and cents. It was right if the deal went right; it was wrong if the deal went wrong.

This spectacle of greed fueled the union rally, where a rabbi took the podium and quoted an ancient Jewish proverb about God rotating the universe so that the star of the rich and unjust falls to the bottom, and the star of the poor and disenfranchised rises to the top: "Soon God will rotate the universe in such a way that the star that's on top will sink to the bottom." I envisioned God reaching out with His hand and suddenly righting an unjust world just as I might reach out and turn an orange in my hand.

I have never been able to shake the Calvinist belief in the depravity of man. I don't believe in everlasting human progress. Instead of moving ever upward and onward and higher, civilizations rise and fall. The star on the top will inevitably plummet to the bottom. And I can't believe, as so many conservatives seem to, that a person's depravity disappears as soon as he begins running a business—that suddenly his pursuit of money will become altruistic as he lives out the virtues of unfettered capitalism, that in seeking success for himself, he will always lift others along with him as a rising tide lifts all boats. Fiscal conservatives may lovingly quote the eighteenth-century economist Adam Smith, who said a business owner is "led by an invisible hand" that guides him into improving society as he seeks his own best interests.[6] When I read "invisible hand," I see more often than not a hand that strangles the weak and defenseless, robbing them to give to the rich. What about "the love of money is a root of all kinds of evil"?[7] What about the Bible's warning that riches have a dirty lure and exert a power that tempts, entraps, and pulls men down into "ruin and destruction"?[8]

The financial crisis cured me of any belief in the morality of the American moneymaking dream. Unfettered avarice brought down a nation while the greedy men still flew corporate jets and doled out million-dollar bonuses to the people who caused the crash. They posted record profits and paid just a few percent in taxes and got billions in bailout funds from US taxpayers, even as 9 percent of Americans suffered jobless in a crisis they didn't create. A monster shoveled jobs and houses and hopes into its maw with that grasping "invisible hand."

CONSERVATIVES ARGUE THAT THIS human tendency toward corruption means that unemployment benefits and government health insurance will make the poor lazy, that they will become food-stamp gobblers with no incentive to work for themselves. But I side with the poor and powerless since—as we've seen—they have far less ability to destroy all our lives. That is why, almost a year after I went to that union protest, I found myself in front of another video camera—this time with my full knowledge. I was helping to organize a demonstration against Bank of America for receiving a $45 billion bailout and yet paying no taxes at all.[9] I told the camera I was protesting the fact that corporations had the lobbying clout to write tax laws with so many loopholes that two-thirds of them paid no taxes and 83 percent of the hundred largest publicly traded corporations could hide their income in offshore tax havens.[10] I was protesting corporate corruption that abused its influence to shape laws for its own benefit while the rest of us faced cuts to education and health aid.

When I finished my interview, I looked around, relieved to see a young man and two middle-aged women standing at the foot of the stairs next to the plaza, bearing cardboard signs. I wouldn't be the lone demonstrator. "She came here for a job interview, and we decided to come too, for the demonstration," one woman told me. She looked around at the empty plaza. "Sure hope there are more people coming."

Me too. None of our "tax-avoidance specialists" were here to give their sarcastic performances advising people how to avoid paying taxes. None of the cheerleaders were here to lead people in cheers. What if it was chaos? What if no one chanted? What if no one printed out the fliers? What if people challenged the police and got themselves arrested and everyone else was confused as to whether they were supposed to get themselves arrested? What if everyone blamed me and my inexperience in organizing an anticorporate demonstration?

But a few more people trickled in and then a few more. Suddenly a crowd assembled on the plaza next to Madison Square Garden, carrying signs that said "Chop from the top" and "Bank of America pays $0 Taxes. How much do you pay?" A lanky lawyer put on a neon green hat so anyone in legal trouble would know to come to him. The guy assigned to crowd control strolled up, looking bleary eyed and clutching a coffee cup. A serious youth approached me. "I have an idea for a cheer, and they said I should tell you: 'BOA, your heart is black! You should give some money back.'"

I repeated it to the "tax-avoidance specialist" who had just walked up, dressed like a wealthy banker and carrying a sign that said "Ask me how to pay $0 in taxes." A white-haired woman holding a big roll of fliers asked me, "What should I say? 'Bank of America doesn't pay its taxes? Don't you think Bank of America should pay its taxes?'"

And suddenly everything was moving. We crossed the street, and 150 people stood next to Bank of America chanting, "BOA must pay! BOA must pay!"

A few weeks before this, when I found myself wondering if it was time to wave a sign again, I thought of all the times I'd done so before and wondered if it did any good—in fact if it actually hindered the cause. How many people grow cynical because activists are more interested in yelling than in giving real aid? Should I forget carrying signs and instead work quietly behind the scenes? Should I take up a sign for a different cause—or give up on causes altogether? What difference would it make either way?

When I sat in a room to plan that demonstration, I heard both sides. Older people who had walked with Martin Luther King Jr. saw activism bring justice. But my co-organizer described how she and her group of gay and lesbian activists had blocked off the Holland Tunnel only to find, when they looked for the coverage, that they'd gotten just a few paragraphs on a back page of the paper. "That was when a lot of us got turned off from activism," she said.

Sometimes the sign carrying and the civil disobedience and the arms linked in defiance and unity works; sometimes it doesn't. I thought of the Old Testament prophets who were, in some ways, the sign holders of ancient times—the ones standing out on the public corners and decrying the injustice and sin of the people and their leaders, urging repentance and then watching their nation backslide yet again. I thought of Isaiah bellowing,

> Woe to those who decree unrighteous decrees,
> Who write misfortune,
> Which they have prescribed
> To rob the needy of justice,
> And to take what is right from the poor of My people,
> That widows may be their prey,
> And that they may rob the fatherless.[11]

And of the prophet Habakkuk warning,

> Woe to him who builds a town with bloodshed,
> Who establishes a city by iniquity![12]

And Zephaniah pronouncing judgment against those who committed injustice,

> Woe to her who is rebellious and polluted,
> To the oppressing city!…
>
> Her princes in her midst are roaring lions;
> Her judges are evening wolves.[13]

Isaiah preached at kings for over sixty years and saw his nation plunged into war despite his warning to repent from injustice and robbery. Habakkuk and Zephaniah preached of conquering armies and coming woe, and there is no record of their favorable reception. But Jonah refused to take a stand because he thought it was useless, only to find when he went to Nineveh that it was not—the city repented after all.

Sometimes I feel as though I'll burst with anger at the world's injustice. Perhaps this is the time to bellow from the street corners, "Woe to those who write unjust laws." The laws may or may not change, but someone has to say something.

Yes, our primary job as Christians is to love people, and we can't love from behind a barricade. But we have other God-given responsibilities too—to fight against those who make unjust decrees, rob the needy, and deprive the poor of their rights. We can make political the things that are political and make spiritual the things that are spiritual. Sin and pain are spiritual—we treat them in a spiritual way. Pray for the sinner. Speak to the sinner. Try to win the businessman from his greed and give him something else to live for. Love the sinner—and not from behind a barricade but face to face. But when injustice, robbery, and inequity are not just individual but institutional, it's time to take a political stand.

The government can't cure sin or heal pain; it can stop robbery and create laws that treat the poor justly. And it's our role to demand that our leaders do so.

As I walked home from the demonstration, my coffee in one hand and my signs tucked under my arm, I remembered shouting down that woman in the coffee shop and how I'd felt that anything less vocal or public would have been cowardly. I felt the same today. I wasn't under any delusions that our signs would radically alter the course of Manhattan—but I had to say it: "Woe to those who prey on the widows and rob the fatherless."

Because God made everyone, and we can't treat human beings that way.

The Lessons That Last

The weather always seems to figure prominently in gay-marriage debates. Reverend John Hagee claimed Hurricane Katrina was the judgment of God come down to halt a New Orleans gay pride parade.[1] When the Evangelical Lutheran Church in America debated the ordination of noncelibate gay clergy, a tornado struck and bent the cross atop their conference center, which the venerable Reformed theologian John Piper interpreted as a "gentle but firm warning to the ELCA and all of us: Turn from the approval of sin."[2]

The "Stand for Marriage" rally in Albany that year was no exception to the weather rule. I woke up at 5:00 a.m. and took the subway to Penn Station so I could take the Amtrak to Albany for the rally. A heavy sky loomed with the kind of pallid drab you would find in a hospital blanket. I reflected that it had rained on a pro-gay-marriage rally I had once covered, and if I were not the kind of Christian who sets little store in mystical signs from heaven, I might consider this God frowning on us all for fighting so much.

The cab driver dropped me at the side of a building with no sign of protestors. As I stepped out and juggled my iPhone to get my bearings, I noticed a group trotting down the opposite side of the street carrying signs. I knew I was in the right place. The giveaway was the kids—so many, so close in age. I saw a pretty mom pulling two little boys in a big plastic wagon, and a dad wearing a flannel shirt and a "Stand for marriage" button, holding two little kids by the hand. One, bundled against the chill and no more than four years old, held in his little fist a sign that said "I want a mommy and a daddy!" I knew these young couples were flush with the responsibility of parenting their children in the admonition of the Lord and had settled ideas of how life would be and how their children would live. These parents wanted their kids to grow up in the safe world they grew up in and not the kind of world they saw today. They put signs in their children's hands to plead with anyone who would listen, "Think of our children. Not just your own rights and what you want today, but what will happen to these children when marriage and family have fallen apart."

They reminded me of my own parents thwarting the schemes of the Enemy, and when I looked at their children, I saw myself, with my own pro-life sign, making a stand for something I knew mattered deeply but without fully understanding why.

I rarely see people like this anymore, and when I see them in New York, I'm always startled that they exist here. I imagine them living underground in their own communities and only emerging when they feel the earth above them quaking, to defend their homes and to fight for what they see as their very survival. When they say the end is near, they mean it, and they are terrified.

The rain had stopped. I stood back at the fringe of the crowd, pulled out my notebook, and started to write. The leader stood before the assembled demonstrators and rejoiced in the sunshine as a sign: "Today He turned off the water spigot, turned off the rain so we could meet!" The state chair of the Conservative Party said gay-marriage advocates "have an intention to destroy organized religion." He shouted, "We cannot let that happen!" He raised the specter of godless Europe.

Ruben Diaz, the Democratic senator who had mobilized opposition to the same-sex marriage bill, called on his Republican counterparts to carry on the cause. In a wild call to undecided Democrats, he echoed what homosexuals say to their own closeted ranks: "Come out! Come out! Come out! Come out! Come out! Come out!" It swelled into another cry: "No gay marriage! No gay marriage! No gay marriage! No gay marriage!" Diaz thundered it and the crowd echoed it and roared back.

A pastor led the crowd in an antiphon, a call and response that echoed down the capitol steps. "In the face of great immorality," he called.

The crowd shouted, "Will You not revive us again?"

"In a nation that wants to throw away the cross and forget its Christian moorings..."

"Will You not revive us again?"

Someone waved a sign that asked "Are we desperate for God?" Another raised a misspelled missive: "Man + Woman = Marriage. Man + Man = Narcissim." Some of the signs' clumsy wording made me squirm: "Tell us—How do gays consummate their marriage? Is that natural?"

They split themselves into four groups and scattered to the north, south, east, and west to pray and petition their legislators, just as I remembered doing when I went to the New Mexico capitol building each year for my training in political worldview. At one time I would have been with them. The pledge to the flag would have stirred me, and I would have been wearing a shirt imprinted with the scripture they were praying: "If My people who are called by My name will humble themselves, and pray and seek My face, and turn from their wicked ways, then I will hear from heaven, and will forgive their sin and heal their land."[3] I would have been praying for and pleading with legislators and considering any mockery I endured a grim vindication of my worth as a Christian soldier.

LOOKING BACK ON THE YEARS that changed me from someone carrying a George W. Bush tote bag to someone protesting corporate greed, from someone who wept with joy at the national anthem to someone who could no longer sing it without a pang of loss—I've wondered what part of me remains. What did my parents teach me that I will pass on to my children?

To care. There was never any question for me, growing up, that we should care what happened in the world. And I still do. I care that the gap between the poor and the rich grows smaller, that the children of the urban underclass get educations that can lift them from poverty, that the rich and powerful stop purchasing politicians, that pregnant women who want to keep their babies get the help they need to do so, that we protect the religious freedom of our Muslim neighbors. As I slog through a polluted stream of news, I hurtle into despair and wish I cared less. I threaten to stop voting, to move to Europe if the outcome of the next election doesn't go according to plan. But I cannot help caring, and I battle the cynicism that would make me stop.

To love. Not just with words but with actions. My parents cared for each of my grandparents to their last day, taking them into our home and nursing them through dementia and cancer, changing colostomy bags, adjusting hospital beds, swabbing cracked lips, holding hands, reading Scripture. My parents adopted two children from Haiti, knowing they would be attending soccer practices and parenting through the years that most people their age spend golfing. These acts of love were more radical and countercultural than anything else they did—a quiet affront to our cultural values of selfishness and materialism. Living these values takes more courage than defending them in the public square. Being pro-family is harder, and more radical, than carrying a sign that says you are.

To take heart. My dad used to tell me, "You could take this county for Christ." That triumphal creed is no longer mine, but I want to retain that sense of optimism with a different sense of mission. Instead of claiming ground and seeking power to dominate and exert my will, I want to live with the kind of love and optimism that is only possible when I hold a vision of the world's ultimate redemption from injustice and suffering. I will be tempted, as Henri J. M. Nouwen warned, to a frenzied pursuit of "upward mobility." But "God's way is not to be relevant, or spectacular, or powerful. God's way is downward. 'Blessed are the humble. Blessed are the poor of heart. Blessed are the meek. Blessed are the peacemakers.'"[4]

In other words, as Jesus urged His followers, "Take heart! I have overcome the world"[5]—not through a show of power but a picture of love.

ACKNOWLEDGMENTS

*T*his book is the product of years of living and so the product of the people who have shaped my character and political views over the years. Thanks to the professors who stretched my mind and gave me a new perspective on life, history, and politics: Dr. Daniel Sundahl, Dr. Mark Kalthoff, and Dr. Richard Gamble. Although I've never met him, the writings of James Davison Hunter encouraged me by giving a much more intelligent and scholarly voice to my own struggle to understand a Christian vision of politics.

I want to thank all the people who believed in me: Mike and Judy Harris, Christine Sutton Akerman, and the many friends who cheered me on. Thanks to my sister Dawn Ogden, who read the very first terrible paragraphs of this book and called them amazing. And thanks to my editor, Laura Barker, who read the terrible first draft of this book and told me it really was not all that amazing.

I thank my husband more than anyone. I first realized I loved him when I knew I couldn't write this book, or accomplish any of my dreams, without him. With his tough-minded editing and an enthusiasm that rallies on despite reading the same chapters and calming the same fears again and again, he proved me right.

NOTES

Prologue: A Firmer Foundation
1. Jeremiah 29:11
2. John 16:33, NIV
3. David Kinnaman and Gabe Lyons, *unChristian: What a New Generation Really Thinks About Christianity...and Why It Matters* (Grand Rapids: Baker, 2007), 155.
4. Kinnaman and Lyons, *unChristian,* 156.
5. Public Religion Research Institute, "The Faith and American Politics Survey: The Young and the Faithful," sponsored by Faith in Public Life, released October 8, 2008.

Chapter 1: Flesh and Blood
1. Proverbs 24:11
2. Jeremiah 31:15, NIV
3. Leviticus 18:22, NIV
4. Romans 1:26–27, KJV
5. Matthew 6:5, NIV
6. Fyodor Dostoevsky, *The Brothers Karamozov* (New York: Modern Library, 1996), 59.
7. Dostoevsky, *The Brothers Karamozov,* 60.
8. Proverbs 24:11

Chapter 2: On Earth as It Is in Heaven

1. Ephesians 6:12, KJV
2. 2 Timothy 1:7
3. See Ephesians 6:16.
4. See Isaiah 11:6.
5. James Davison Hunter, *To Change the World: The Irony, Tragedy, and Possibility of Christianity in the Late Modern World* (New York: Oxford University Press, 2010).
6. Julie Watson, "Christian Conservatives Target Seated Judges," Associated Press, May 30, 2010.
7. Lady Gaga, interview by Larry King, *Larry King Live,* CNN, June 1, 2010, http://transcripts.cnn.com/TRANSCRIPTS/1006/01/lkl.01.html.
8. Isaiah 11:4, 6, 9

Chapter 3: Of Goats and Sheep

1. Theodore Roosevelt, "Citizenship in a Republic" (speech, Sorbonne, Paris, April 23, 1910), www.bartleby.com/56/4.html.
2. Matthew 10:34
3. Joshua 24:15

Chapter 4: The Shining City's Superman

1. See 1 Peter 3:15.
2. Luke 4:18, NIV
3. See Isaiah 55:11.
4. Ronald Reagan, "Farewell Address to the Nation,"

January 11, 1989, The American Presidency Project, Santa Barbara, CA, www.presidency.ucsb.edu/ws/?pid =29650.

5. John 18:36

6. Matthew 5

Chapter 5: While God Is Marching On

1. Leonard Pitts Jr., "We'll Go Forward from This Moment," *Miami Herald,* September 12, 2001.

2. See Matthew 6:6, KJV.

3. David Barton, *America's Godly Heritage* (Aledo, TX: WallBuilders, 1992–96), 2 sound cassettes, www .metacafe.com/watch/6063727/removal_of_prayer _from_school_the_devastating_effect_barton.

4. Deuteronomy 30:15, 19, NIV

5. John Winthrop, "A Model of Christian Charity" (1630), quoted in Francis J. Bremer, *John Winthrop: America's Forgotten Founding Father* (New York: Oxford University Press, 2003), 92–93.

6. Reinhold Niebuhr, *The Irony of American History* (Chicago: University of Chicago Press, 1952), xxiv.

Chapter 6: Deliver Us from Evil

1. Wilfred Owen, "Dulce et Decorum Est," quoted in *The Complete Poems and Fragments Of Wilfred Owen,* ed. Jon Stallworthy (London: Chatto and Windus, 1983), First World War Poetry Digital Archive, www.oucs.ox.ac.uk/ ww1lit/collections/item/3303.

2. "I'll Be Seeing You," by Sammy Fain and Irving Kahal, 1938.

3. "When the Lights Go On Again," by Eddie Seller, Sol Marcus, and Bennie Benjamin, 1942.

4. "(There'll Be Bluebirds Over) The White Cliffs of Dover," by Nat Burton and Walter Kent, 1941.

5. Matthew 22:21, kjv

6. Nick Davies, Jonathan Steele, and David Leigh, "Iraq War Logs: Secret Files Show How US Ignored Torture," *Guardian,* October 22, 2010, www.guardian.co.uk/world/2010/oct/22/iraq-war-logs-military-leaks/print.

7. Sabrina Tavernise and Andrew W. Lehren, "Detainees Fared Worse in Iraqi Hands, Logs Say," *New York Times,* October 22, 2010, www.nytimes.com/2010/10/23/world/middleeast/23detainees.html.

8. Wilfred Owen, *The Collected Poems of Wilfred Owen,* ed. Edmund Blunden (New York: New Directions, 1963), 160, 162.

Chapter 7: Holes

1. Peggy Noonan, *What I Saw at the Revolution: A Political Life in the Reagan Era* (New York: Random House, 2003), 357.

Chapter 8: Judge Not

1. Dan Cox, "Young White Evangelicals: Less Republican, Still Conservative," Pew Forum on Religion and Public Life, September 28, 2007, http://pewforum

.org/Politics-and-Elections/Young-White-Evangelicals-
Less-Republican-Still-Conservative.aspx.

2. Matt Kaufman, "Gays vs. the Garden Guy," *Boundless
Webzine,* November 30, 2006, www.boundless.org/2005/
articles/a0001402.cfm.

Chapter 9: A More Perfect Union

1. Andrew Sullivan, "Goodbye to All That: Why Obama
Matters," *Atlantic,* December 2007, www.theatlantic
.com/magazine/archive/2007/12/goodbye-to-all-that-
why-obama-matters/6445.

2. Barack Obama, speaking at Saddleback Presidential
Candidates Forum, August 16, 2008, CNN.com,
http://transcripts.cnn.com/TRANSCRIPTS/0808/16/
se.02.html.

3. Abraham Lincoln, "First Inaugural Address," *Inaugural
Addresses of the Presidents of the United States* (Washington
DC: US GPO, 1989; Bartleby.com, 2001), www.bartleby
.com/124/pres31.html.

4. Sullivan, "Goodbye to All That," *Atlantic.*

Chapter 10: An Ear to Hear

1. Jessamyn West, "The Day of the Hawk," in *Collected
Stories of Jessamyn West* (New York: Harcourt Brace
Jovanovich, 1986), 402–13.

2. West, *Collected Stories,* 412.

3. "2007 Country Reports on Human Rights Practices:
Afghanistan," US Department of State, Bureau of

Democracy, Human Rights, and Labor, March 11, 2008, www.state.gov/g/drl/rls/hrrpt/2007/100611.htm#.

4. Austin Ruse, "Kosovar Refugee Women 'Just Say No': Milosevic Invites UNFPA to Target Kosovo Population upon Their Return Home," *PRI Review* 9, no. 4 (June–July 1999), www.pop.org/content/kosovar-refugee-women-just-say-no-1526.

5. Austin Ruse, "Pro-Life Naïfs in the Big City," *Catholic Thing*, October 27, 2010, www.thecatholicthing.org/columns/2010/pro-life-naifs-in-the-big-city.html.

6. James Davison Hunter, *Before the Shooting Begins: Searching for Democracy in America's Culture War* (New York: Free Press, 1994), 232.

Chapter 11: Our Daily Bread

1. See 2 Thessalonians 3:10.

2. Matthew 25:42

3. You can find samples of the artwork of Gabriel Reese at www.specterart.com.

Chapter 12: Treasure in Heaven

1. Although my footage never aired, the episode that did air can be found at http://abcnews.go.com/WhatWouldYou Do/video/nanny-abuse-intervene-6800329.

2. Proverbs 24:11

3. Proverbs 24:12, NIV

4. Steve Eder and Karey Wutkowski, "Goldman's 'Fabulous' Fab's Conflicted Love Letters," Reuters, April 26, 2010,

www.reuters.com/article/2010/04/26/us-goldman-
emails-idUSTRE63O26E20100426.

5. Daniel Sparks, quoted in "Goldman Sachs Execs Get
   Grilled on the Hill," *Nightly Business Report*, PBS, April
   27, 2010, www.pbs.org/nbr/site/onair/transcripts/
   goldman_sachs_execs_grilled_on_the_hill_100427.

6. Adam Smith, *The Theory of Moral Sentiments*, 6th ed.
   (London: A. Millar, 1759), IV.I.10.

7. 1 Timothy 6:10

8. 1 Timothy 6:9, NIV

9. Christopher Helman, "What the Top U.S. Companies
   Pay in Taxes," Forbes.com, April 1, 2010, www.forbes
   .com/2010/04/01/ge-exxon-walmart-business-washington-
   corporate-taxes.html.

10. "International Taxation: Large U.S. Corporations and
    Federal Contractors with Subsidiaries in Jurisdictions
    Listed as Tax Havens or Financial Privacy Jurisdictions,"
    US Government Accountability Office, GAO-09-157,
    December 18, 2008.

11. Isaiah 10:1–2

12. Habakkuk 2:12

13. Zephaniah 3:1, 3

Epilogue: The Lessons That Last

1. John Hagee, quoted in Terry Gross, "Pastor John Hagee
   on Christian Zionism, Katrina," *Fresh Air from WHYY,*
   broadcast September 18, 2006, www.npr.org/templates/
   story/story.php?storyId=90508742.

2. John Piper, "The Tornado, the Lutherans, and Homosexuality," *Desiring God* (blog), August 19, 2009, www .desiringgod.org/blog/posts/the-tornado-the-lutherans-and-homosexuality.

3. 2 Chronicles 7:14

4. Henri J. M. Nouwen, *From Fear to Love: Lenten Reflections on the Parable of the Prodigal Son,* The Henri Nouwen Legacy Trust, 5.

5. John 16:33, NIV